LOSING

FELICITAS

ALSO BY REBEKAH HEPPNER

The Lost Leaders: How Corporate America Loses Women Leaders

(New York: Palgrave MacMillan, 2013)

LOSING FELICITAS

A Story of Growing Up, Catholic School, and White Flight in Chicago

Rebekah Heppner

First Edition
ISBN: 978-0-578-48719-9

Cover Photo: My Last Look at St. Felicitas Church, July 1, 2018

For information contact:
LosingFelicitas@gmail.com

This book is dedicated to all the parishioners of
St. Felicitas Parish, 1919–2019.

CONTENTS

PART TWO – MY RESEARCH

Acknowledgements

Thank you to my sisters for sharing their memories of growing up, even though we seem to have had three completely different childhoods—especially in how we remember our last few years in Chicago.

I'd also like to thank everyone else who shared their memories of St. Felicitas with me. I have worked hard to protect your identities, so I will not name you here, but you know who you are. Your memories helped me recall our years together more clearly and in richer detail. This book would not have been possible without you.

Foreword

This is a work of nonfiction. Everything in Part One is true to the best of my memory or based on memories of my classmates, as told to me. Our memories are not infallible, especially fifty years later. If you went to St. Felicitas School, or lived in Avalon Park, and you remember this era or these events differently, please know that I have told the story as I remember it and have not intentionally distorted any facts.

I've created four composite characters to share my friends' stories and given them the pseudonyms Beth, Eileen, Laura and Sheila. Details about their families and homes have also been changed. Other children in this book have also been given pseudonyms.

Introduction

COMING OF AGE IN THE AGE OF WHITE FLIGHT

This is a book about moving—moving away from a neighborhood on the South Side of Chicago in 1969, during the time known as "white flight." It is also about loss; the loss we felt as children, being forced (by our parents) to leave our cherished childhood neighborhood at what to us was the worst possible time, our early teen years. But it is not the usual story of white flight—white families leaving neighborhoods quickly once a black family moves in. Our families wanted to stay and live in what was now an integrated community. But, little by little, we kids began to live in fear of being physically attacked while we were doing the things we had always done – going to the park, walking to school, hanging out at our neighborhood candy store. Although our attackers were black, they weren't the African-American children who went to Catholic school with us. But the attacks happened near our school, our church and our homes. Eventually, our parents made the difficult decision to move, reluctantly, to someplace where they felt they could keep us safe.

White families started moving away from my neighborhood in the early 1960s. I can only assume some of them moved because they did not want to live with blacks. I was too young to ask them. I do remember hearing about "blockbusters," people going door to door to scare homeowners into moving, by telling them their property values were about to go down, because the neighborhood was "changing." But my family, and those of my closest friends, stayed, at least for awhile. We were not the first to join into the white flight. Our parents were teaching us, both by their words and their actions, that we could live in an integrated neighborhood.

Incorporated into my memories in Part One are the memories of a small group of women who attended all nine years of grammar school with me and are still my friends today. We were all born in 1954, and remember an idyllic early childhood, as well as the fear and violence we gradually came to accept as a normal part of our lives. The neighborhood may have been a dangerous place for black children who moved there in the early sixties, but, by the late sixties, it was not safe for white children either.

My family eventually did move, as did those of all of my white friends, not for fear of living next to black families, but for the safety of their children. Fifty years later, I am still troubled both by my memories of that time and how it is reflected in history. As the sixties moved into the history books, it seems to me that white flight has been attributed mostly to white racists, and their actions are blamed for the degradation of many of the neighborhoods they fled. Yet my friends and I recall our parents and teachers imparting anti-racist beliefs to us. Our story adds another layer to the traditional narrative of white flight.

Felicitas is the name of the saint to which our church and school were dedicated, and "felicitas" reflects what we lost—it means blessed, happy. To us kids, moving away felt like losing the sense of blessed happiness we had living in our parish. It was not a loss that cost us much in the long run; our families had the freedom and resources to move to "better" neighborhoods, many to brand-new homes in the suburbs. Our families did not face discrimination or unwelcoming neighbors when they moved into their new homes. Black families faced both of those in many neighborhoods in Chicago and had faced that and worse for generations.

The residents of our neighborhood, and of many of those surrounding us, organized to try to work through the "transition," in hopes that they could continue to enjoy the sense of community that had attracted them to the neighborhood in the first place. But we kids were not aware of any of that. We just wanted to enjoy our childhood, and live near our friends, and attend our church and school. We lost something meaningful to us, and it is part of who we are today. The loss was compounded by our adolescence, a time when everything feels so important, so personal.

Over the years, I have learned more about what was happening in the world, and on Chicago's South Side, during the

1960s. I was somewhat aware of the larger events that were occurring around us, but my worldview was that of a child. While writing this book, I took the time to research a few subjects that caught my interest. Although my research is not comprehensive, it does provide important context to my story, so I've shared it in Part Two. First, I wanted to understand why there were so many black families wanting to live in St. Felicitas parish, and the surrounding Avalon Park neighborhood, at that particular time in history. Second, I was curious about the neighborhood associations that were working to achieve what they called "successful integration." Third, I wanted to learn how the Catholic Church was involved in this difficult time, and how Vatican II might have impacted their involvement. Lastly, I wanted to know more about the street gangs nearby, which influenced the violence we were experiencing in our neighborhood.

As a child, I knew that the headquarters of the notorious Blackstone Rangers street gang and those mammoth public housing towers, the Robert Taylor Homes, were nearby, within a few miles of our school and church. Further away, but in our living rooms every night, the Vietnam War dominated the news with its daily body counts. Our long-anticipated eighth-grade year would be marred by the assassinations of The Reverend Dr. Martin Luther King, Jr. and Senator Robert Kennedy. And it didn't stop then. The unpopularity of the war would lead to the violence, also in Chicago and not far from my home, at the 1968 Democratic Convention, a few weeks after our graduation. It was a tumultuous time but, then again, we grew up under that constant threat of annihilation, the Cold War, with a fallout shelter sign prominently displayed on our school building.

It sometimes amazes me that I remember my childhood as idyllic, considering the prevailing sense of doom that surrounded us. For that I thank my parents and teachers and, of course, my dear childhood friends. This is their story, too.

PART ONE

MY MEMORIES

Prologue

MY LAST WALK HOME

When someone asks me to name events that shaped my life, this is always number one: In August of 1969, we moved from our family home in the St. Felicitas parish on the South Side of Chicago to a new life in Oklahoma City. I started kindergarten at my parish grammar school in the fall of 1959 and graduated from eighth grade there. We moved after my first year at an all-girls Catholic high school nearby. I was 15. It wasn't a choice I made. It wasn't really a choice my parents made. Well, the Oklahoma City part was their choice, but the timing was not. My girlfriends were all moving to other parts of the greater Chicagoland area within a year or so of our move date, several to the Beverly neighborhood to the west, some to the south suburbs. One good friend, whose father worked downtown, moved to a suburb on the North Side, which seemed pretty exotic to us. Then there was my family, moving to Oklahoma.

It may sound odd, but I grew up always knowing we would move to Oklahoma. As a small child, I never thought it would be such a significant event in my life. I probably didn't even realize it, "moving to Oklahoma," was a real thing. We had visited there a few times; my grandparents and aunt and uncle lived there, my mother's family. She grew up in Oklahoma. My parents met around the end of World War II. My dad was stationed at Camp Maxey, which was near my mother's home town of Atoka. Lots of geographically-diverse couples got their start that way at the end of the war. The family lore, as I internalized it, was that Dad promised Mom he would take her back to Oklahoma one day. I can only imagine how much she did not like Chicago's South Side—the bitter winters, the busy streets, the grime from the steel mills—so different from her small-town upbringing. It was my misfortune that the day my dad actually made good on his promise came when I was 15. But again, the timing was not his choice, at least not completely.

On the day before we left, a beautiful summer day, Mark Peterson and I walked together from the playground at St. Felicitas School, by then commonly known among us teenagers as "The Grounds," to our respective homes on Dorchester Avenue. He was not "walking me home"; that was a very different thing. We just happened to be walking at the same time in the same direction, as I headed home for the very last time. The walk between our school and my house is one long city block and three short ones, about a quarter mile. Between the first day of kindergarten in the fall of 1959 and this day, ten years later, I walked those four blocks nearly 2,000 times—each way. I can see it all in my head still, the long block nearest my house was often darkened by the shade of large trees, combined with the typical Chicago overcast skies. There weren't many children on that block, so it seemed scarier than others. And it got scarier as the years progressed. Anything could happen in this formerly safe neighborhood of ours. Groups of black teens, boys or girls, might come out from the gangways between houses or the bushes, taunting us and chasing us. Older black teens had been seen walking down the middle of the street with chains and baseball bats. They weren't our African-American classmates; we rarely knew who they were, but we knew their goal – to scare us.

But the day of my last walk home was sunny and bright; the block didn't seem scary at all. Perhaps Chicago was mocking us for deciding we had to leave it. The beautiful trees on our street were bright green, and the dappled shade they created on the sidewalk is still vivid in my memory. This is probably the first memory I intentionally created, to keep and recall for the rest of my life. When we got to the Peterson house, Mark asked me, quite sincerely, if I thought I would ever come back to Chicago. I was shocked by the suggestion that I would not return. It was my home. That is when it hit me: my "home" would not be there to return to. Our neighborhood would never be the same. All of my white friends had either moved away or were going to move soon. A handful of white families in the parish, including Mark's, stayed a couple more years, but the neighborhood was no longer a safe place for children, including us teenagers. The idyllic parish of our childhood had been replaced by a gritty urban landscape where we, white Catholic school kids, felt like prey for those who seemed to want to scare us, for reasons we didn't understand.

I walked the rest of the way a bit slower, realizing now the significance of my steps. The next morning my dad and I would hit the road in his '68 Cadillac Eldorado. I'm sure there were moving trucks involved at some point, but I wasn't in charge of this move and did not sweat the details. I knew that my mom was following a few weeks later with one of my sisters, her husband and their baby, and my dad would be returning to our house, where my other sister and brother-in-law would live with him for several more months. I don't think our house was even on the market. He still owned his grocery store. These were obviously difficult times for my parents. But I was 15; what mattered to me were my friends—and there they were, on the sidewalk next to our old red brick bungalow, as I drove away with my dad. This one is not a pretty picture in my head: me, reduced to tears, my father's heart no doubt breaking, my friends, waving and calling out their goodbyes, all of us wondering if we would ever see each other again.

ST. FELICITAS PARISH

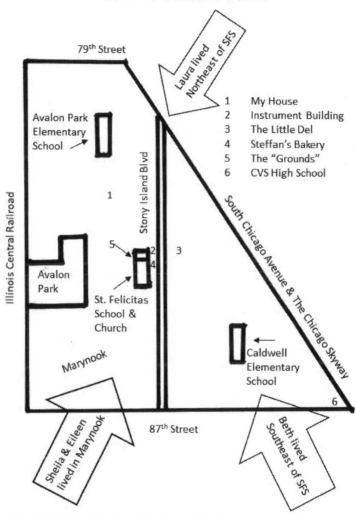

Laura lived Northeast of SFS

79th Street

Avalon Park Elementary School

Stony Island Blvd

Illinois Central Railroad

Avalon Park

St. Felicitas School & Church

Marynook

87th Street

South Chicago Avenue & The Chicago Skyway

Caldwell Elementary School

Beth lived Southeast of SFS

Sheila & Eileen lived in Marynook

1   My House
2   Instrument Building
3   The Little Del
4   Steffan's Bakery
5   The "Grounds"
6   CVS High School

Map hand drawn by the author. Size and scale are as I remember them.
Distance from 79th St to 87th St is one mile – although it seemed farther.

Chapter 1

OUR EARLY YEARS AT ST. FELICITAS

Kindergarten

I was in the afternoon kindergarten at St. Felicitas. When my sisters, who were seven and twelve years old, came home for lunch on their first day of school in the fall of 1959, I was proudly dressed in my brand-new uniform—a powder blue dress with flouncy bloomers to match and a starched white pinafore. My grandmother was living with us at the time and made my uniform on her old Singer sewing machine; I didn't have to wear a hand-me-down from my sisters, like so many of my classmates. Most of us had older sisters and, well, "waste not, want not" was big in our parish. We loved those uniforms so much that my friend Beth sometimes wore hers on the weekend. We were really quite cute in those kindergarten frocks. I can show you the pictures.

That first day, I was quite excited, but my sisters still needed to eat. We came home for lunch every day; our school did not have a cafeteria. Lunch at our house was usually something along the lines of Campbell's canned tomato soup and egg salad sandwiches, cut into triangles, a specialty of my mother's. If you got the rounded edges of the bread on your triangle, you could rock it like a rocking horse. Not that we ever played with our food. After lunch that first day, we all walked to school together. My mother was even with us this time, being that it was my first-ever day in school. My seven-year-old sister would be in charge of walking me starting day two. We walked that one long city block and three short ones, then we were helped across a very busy street by Mrs. Mitchell, our crossing guard. I know Mrs. Mitchell meant well, but sometimes her ushering us across four lanes of traffic felt a little like being dragged through an amusement park fun house, fast. She could get across four lanes of traffic in under a minute, holding the hands of four or five little kids, blowing her whistle, and glaring at the waiting cars that seemed ready to pounce on us.

I was *so* very happy to finally get to go to school, like my sisters, but I'll admit I was also a little bit scared. I had no idea what to expect; I'd never been in a group setting like a school before. My mom was of the "stay-at-home" variety, like most of the moms I knew. Our usual after-lunch activity was watching Bozo's Circus (a true Chicago treasure), followed by The Doctors and Days of Our Lives. Soap operas weren't as graphic back then, or maybe I just didn't understand them.

My sisters left us to join their classmates on the playground in front of the main school building, while Mom walked with me into the building next door, right to the entrance of the kindergarten. My mother had a very distinctive mole on her lower leg. I can still see it clearly in that moment—nearly eye level from my five-year-old's vantage point—as she turned to walk *away* from me. What?! She was leaving me? I was devastated. I had only been separated from her once in my entire five years and six months of life. She made a trip to Oklahoma when her father died. I was just three then and my dad stayed home with me and my sisters. That was certainly traumatic but did not in any way prepare me to be abandoned in the dark hallway of an old building, outside a room filled with five-year-old strangers—and one very large nun. (She was probably about five foot two, but that was a lot bigger than me.) I barely knew what a nun was; I'd only seen them across our crowded church on Sundays. This one was completely covered in dark blue wool with white cardboard around her face and over her chest and a black veil over her head. You could barely see her face. She was wearing heavy black shoes, more like boots, that could squash a little kid like me. In the face of this life-altering moment, my mother just turned and walked away. Completely distraught, I burst into tears. The nun, who turned out to be very nice most of the time, and extremely patient, tried to comfort me and somehow got me to join some other little girls sitting on the carpet in the middle of a brightly lit room. She eventually joined us there, sitting in a chair and talking calmly, reading to us. There were other teary-eyed girls there, too; it was a tough day for us all. Eventually, we settled down to listen to the story she was reading, probably something about a saint.

Turns out, kindergarten was amazing. As soon as I relaxed a bit, I felt a lot better, because the room was really great. It wasn't like the traditional classrooms we would spend the following eight years in and was separate from the "big kids" in the main school building. We were in the old church that was remodeled when our new one opened a few years before. The men of our parish (we knew them as the "dads") volunteered to make the renovations. Built in the early twenties, this small building originally housed the old church (where I was baptized), the entire school and a convent. It now held a full-sized gym, two first-grade classrooms, and our own, very special kindergarten space.

Once you got through the dark and dreary hallway, the room was large, bright and colorful. There were tables on one end for crafts and play areas on the opposite end—boys on the first level with tools for banging on things, girls on the second level with dolls for pretending to keep house. There were no boys around on that first day, though; we were to be kept separate for the first week. The day the boys joined us, we girls were already in the room, playing quietly, when the boys came running in and headed right for the boys' area—loudly. I didn't have brothers; this was my first exposure to boys my age. I wasn't afraid of them so much as just startled at how loud they were and how fast they moved.

In between the single-sex play areas and the craft tables on the other end of the room was a vast open area—it needed to be big, there were forty of us in there at a time. One nun. Forty five-year-olds. Really. We would sit for many hours on the rug where I was taken that first day. Sister Mary Anthony would read to us and teach us important things one needed to know to be ready for the big move across the hall to first grade the following year.

Sister Mary Anthony also taught us to sing in French (Frère Jacques) and to make little animals and small dishes out of clay. We had a real kiln in our kindergarten classroom. My first attempt at a dish was an olive-green ash tray for my mom, who was a chain smoker. I drew the veins of a leaf into it with a toothpick. It really looked a little like a leaf, if you used your imagination. While taking our artwork out of the kiln, mine was broken. Probably by me, but I blame Sister Mary Anthony. Who lets a five-year-old handle priceless pottery? She let me make another one, but it was a rush job and never lived up to the beauty of that first attempt.

Our class put on a play that year about a little red hen, to show off our amazing acting and singing abilities to our parents. Laura, who was the smallest kid in our class, had the lead—the little red hen herself. She remembers being quite serious about it and very proud of her performance. As one of ten children in the McDonald family, she probably didn't get too many chances to be the center of attention.

If you check out our kindergarten class picture, to see how cute we all were in those uniforms, you will see one little girl on the front row looking kind of sad and sporting two black eyes. That is my friend Sheila. The day before our class picture was taken, Sheila was riding in her family's car with her mother. We rode up front without seat belts in the fifties. When they pulled up at their house, instead of getting out of the passenger side, Sheila crawled over to get out on the driver's side. Her mother slammed the heavy old car door—right on Sheila's little nose. It was, of course, an accident, and I'm sure her mom felt horrible about it. Not bad enough to keep her home, though, she had toddlers to contend with there, so Sheila's mother's accident is immortalized in our class photo. Child protection would be called if a kid turned up in school like that now.

My sister Terry remembers a bad experience she and I had on our walk to school one day that year. She was supposed to walk with me, being two years older, remember? She knew that, but she was walking a few yards ahead on this particular day, chatting with one of her girlfriends. They saw razor blades lying on the sidewalk—just lying there, unpackaged, uncovered, sharp razor blades. She claims that she yelled back to me to be careful and *not* to touch them. I have no memory of this at all, despite the fact I ended up bleeding. She tells me we ran to school together, me crying and her worrying, not about me, but about how much trouble she was going to get into. She was supposed to be my protector. She thinks the people who lived in the house where the razor blades were found didn't like children and put the razor blades there to keep us from walking by their house. That sounds far-fetched to me, but I can't think of any other reason why there would be razor blades on the sidewalk in our residential neighborhood. Not in 1959 anyway.

My friend Eileen has very clear memories of a competition, toward the end of our kindergarten year, to learn a speech that had very grown-up words in it. The first child to correctly recite it would give the speech at a school assembly. Eileen still remembers the opening line: "Dear Reverend Fathers, on behalf of my esteemed colleagues and myself." Kids must have spent hours practicing, their mothers and siblings helping them to memorize the speech; we wouldn't learn to read for another year. It turned out that two girls had it memorized at the same time, so they presented it together. Eileen was one of the winners, which is probably why she remembers this so well. Her chance to shine came at one of the numerous school assemblies we would be a part of during our grade school years. Monsignor Walsh, the head of our parish during my entire time there, was present, along with Fathers Kelley and O'Donnell; they were the "Reverend Fathers" being addressed. The school marching band played, the girls' choral sang; there was always lots of pomp at those assemblies. The two kindergarten girls were up on a stage, at a podium, to recite the speech. I'm sure it was a crowd pleaser, two little kindergarteners using all those big words.

But kindergarten eventually ended and, sadly, we had to give up our cute pinafores. Starting in first grade we were mandated to don the more serious and severe uniforms, dark blue serge jumpers over white blouses, that we would wear until a more modern version was introduced. We had to concede our beloved kindergarten classroom, too. There was another group of five-year-olds anxious to start their own grade-school adventures.

Our first-grade classroom was still in the separate, "little people's" building, (that's what our first-grade nun called us, "little people"), but it was set up just like the classrooms the older kids were in—ram-rod straight rows of hard wooden desks with hard wooden bench seats attached to them by wrought iron braces. I suppose the desks and seats got bigger as we did, but so did our class sizes, as our parish was growing for the first few years we were in grade school. One of our two first-grade classrooms was crammed full with 53 kids. In second through fourth grade, some of us had to be put in "split" classrooms, sharing with kids a year older than us, because we couldn't all fit into the standard two rooms per grade. It was still crowded and, with only one nun in charge, the crowdedness left just a little bit of room for goofing off. You had to be brave to misbehave, though; the penalties doled out by the nuns could be harsh.

My Mayberry

That feeling of safety we experienced in kindergarten lasted for the next couple of years; we somehow had the feeling of living in a small town, kind of like the one we saw each week on The Andy Griffith Show, but right there on the South Side of Chicago. My Mayberry centered on the block that included our church, school, gym, playground and the places where the priests (rectory) and nuns (convent) lived. The parish covered about one square mile around that block and was made up of city streets and brick houses but, to us kids, it was a vast, unexplored territory. Before kindergarten, and for a couple of summers afterward, we had to stay on our own block, even side streets were not to be crossed without an adult holding your hand. Starting with kindergarten, we had to cross streets to walk to school, with an older sibling, of course. Eventually you could make the walk alone, but there were always other kids on their way at the same time; there was very little true alone time in those grammar school years, with nearly a thousand school-aged kids in that one square mile. And that doesn't count the "publics," those kids who did not attend St. Felicitas (the

12

Catholics).

Most families in our parish had lots of kids, and we all knew each other's siblings and parents. There were always parish activities going on, traditions that made us feel part of something much bigger than ourselves or our families. I thought this was how life was for everyone, since I had never known anything different. I also thought it would go on this way forever. As I got older, I expected to participate in all the rights of passage I watched my older sisters go through—First Communion, Confirmation, cheerleading, graduation and, one day, a wedding in our beautiful neo-gothic church.

The Martyr and Her Seven Sons

Our church, both the sanctuary itself and the ever-versatile church basement, was a central focus of much of our parish activities, starting with the most traditional—the Catholic mass. Like all good churchgoing families, we got up early on Sunday every week, dressed up and attended mass. I sat with my mom until I got into first grade, then I got to sit with my classmates. My dad was an usher, so he stayed in the back of the church, where he could make sure the teenage boys didn't sneak out. He also helped pass the collection basket and stayed after mass to help the priests count the money. We knew this meant he was one of the most trusted parishioners, in the early years at least. Families with very small children sometimes had to sit in the "cry room," a soundproof room at the back of the church with a glass wall in front to allow the adults to see the mass. I've often found myself wishing there were such quiet rooms in restaurants.

A graduate from 1960 recalled that the parish dads had gone door to door on Sundays to gather pledges for the funds to build this church. It replaced the old church, now the gym/kindergarten building in 1955. On Sunday evenings, if the dads had met their fundraising goal, the church bells would ring at six o'clock, signaling that there would be no school the next day. She recalled hearing children cheering up and down her block when they heard those bells. I wonder if the moms were quite as excited.

I probably have a better picture of our church in my memory than of any home I have ever lived in. I have seen beautiful churches across the country as well as in Europe. I know a pretty church when I see one. Ours was really beautiful. While I was writing this book, it was announced that the Archdiocese of Chicago was closing our beloved parish and combining it with a larger one nearby (which was the home of our archrivals during my grade school years). Over the years, membership at St. Felicitas has declined, and the archdiocese can no longer financially support the many parishes that were needed during the 1960s. I cannot express how sad this makes me feel, despite the fact that I am no longer Catholic, much less attending mass at St. Felicitas.

These early years were all pre-Vatican II, so the priests faced away from us during the mass and spoke in Latin, except for some readings and the sermon. I loved the ritual of the Latin mass; it still represents a "real" church service to me, but, honestly, the incomprehensible language and lack of eye contact made it difficult for us kids to pay attention. And Sunday was not our only trip to church. Starting in first grade, every school day began with a mass that was just slightly shorter than Sunday's mass. I repeat, **every school day.**

Picture nearly a thousand kids, between the ages of six and 14, inside a church with less than 20 adults, mostly nuns. It could have been chaos, but we were scared of those nuns. Spanking was allowed (and practiced) and our parents **always** sided with the nuns. So, we struggled to stay quiet. Much time was spent studying the church's twenty-eight stained-glass windows that showed saints and their symbols in vivid colors. Those windows must have been ten feet tall and were allegedly brought over from France. Below them, the fourteen Stations of the Cross were represented in mosaics inside small panels, surrounded by polished wood paneling. The walls above the stations and around the windows were concrete, the floors were waxed stone and there were huge lights hanging from the beams on the high vaulted ceiling that looked to me to be too heavy to stay up. They were long glass pendant lamps stuck on wooden beams that had been somehow painted with gold leaf flowers. Behind the altar was a relief of St. Felicitas and her seven sons. I cannot even estimate how many times I counted those sons! The story was that she was a martyr and had to watch all seven of her sons killed before her. I don't remember why, probably just for being Catholic. There was a beautiful red stained-glass rose window over her, mirrored by a blue one at the back of the church. The altar and the floor around it were made of marble, from Carrara, where Michelangelo found the stone for sculpting David. The altar was surrounded by a short marble "fence," where parishioners would kneel to receive communion directly from a priest, old style—hands folded, mouth open. Even when the rules for communion changed and most churches removed such railings, ours stayed in place. It had been dedicated to our pastor's mother.

On either side of the main altar was a smaller altar. One had a marble statue of Mary and the other one of Joseph, also marble. Mary was on the left, where the bride's family sits during a wedding. There were usually flowers of some sort, depending on the season. None of the kitschy banners you see in churches today. During Lent all the statues were draped in purple cloth, creating a very creepy feeling, which I guess was the point. Our church seemed huge to us then. Unlike other childhood places, it felt just as huge when I went back as an adult.

There were no sermons on weekdays, so the mass only took about twenty minutes. While we were there, the smell of sugar was almost overwhelming. The tradition, for the kids who could afford it, was to go to Steffan's Bakery before church and buy something to eat at your desk after mass. Those of us who were old enough to take Communion had to fast in the morning, of course. We weren't allowed in the school building until mass was over, so those little white bakery bags were stored right in the pews, on the floor by the kneelers. I guess it saved our moms some time – no one had to make breakfast, but some kids brought their breakfast from home. We felt sorry for them.

Our bakery was in the same square block as the church, but

in the opposite corner. If you were last in line you might have to run all the way to church. Arriving late was frowned upon. When entering the bakery, one found two fairly frazzled women behind the counter and dozens of kids, more than the fire department would ever approve, packed into the small space in front of it. It was loud in there, as kids were calling out their orders, and talking with their friends while they waited their turns. I can still smell it. Every once in a while, since that time, I've stepped into a bakery with that same, very specific smell: sugar, butter, batter—baking in the oven or recently moved to the display cases. Somehow, they mixed together to cause it to smell, well, heavenly. My standard order at the bakery was chocolate milk and two chocolate chip donuts, which cost me 26 cents. I cannot even imagine calling that breakfast today, especially not for children. Maybe the kids that brought their breakfast had parents who were perfectly capable of buying donuts; they just preferred their children to have something nutritious. But as an eight or nine-year-old, the prospect of digging in to those donuts at my school desk helped get me through the unintelligible mass and the boredom of staring at those same statues and windows day in and day out.

The Concrete Jungle

After a quick walk home for lunch, those of us who made it back in time would play on the playground across the street from the school building. We didn't have recess or gym class, but, if we hurried, we could get a good fifteen minutes of outdoor play in after lunch. Our playground was a concrete lot, much like a parking lot, which is what it is today. It had a merry-go-round, monkey bars, slide and swing set, all made of metal. If you fell off one of them you would get scraped up, maybe even bleed. This was not considered a problem by anyone, just part of growing up. Our swings had flat wooden seats, perfect for standing on. If you pumped your legs while standing, you could fly really high. I never fell off the swings, but I remember a few mishaps on the merry-go-round when it was full of kids. The boys took turns running in the middle, pushing the center bars, and running on the outside, pulling on the handles. If the ratio of pushers and pullers to riders was high, it got going really fast. There was probably some physics involved, having to do with relative weight, but I knew you were not supposed to annoy those pushing or they might go even faster, increasing your chances of getting thrown off by the sheer speed of the thing. Coming down the slide was an even more likely time to hit the hard pavement. The goal was to land on your feet, but that didn't always happen. Next to the playground was an open lot filled with gravel that could be used when we needed a "field" for dodge ball or if the boys wanted to throw a football. Falling on that lot was even more treacherous.

When it was time for lunch period to end and school to start, two bells rang. At the first bell we were to "freeze" wherever we were—not so easy if you were on your way down the slide or in the midst of falling off the merry-go-round. The second bell meant we could, quietly, walk to our class's designated spot to line up. We also used the playground after school and in the summer. I remember one summer doing flips on the monkey bars so much that I had bruises on my stomach. As we got older, the playground became a place to hang out after school, especially for the teenage boys in our neighborhood.

Parental Involvement, circa 1962

In addition to attending mass with us on Sundays, our parents were very involved in the church and school. They attended many, many school programs—plays, recitals, open houses—as well as helping to stage other parish events like fish fries and turkey raffles (our annual fundraiser). The Mother's Club held bake sales and pot luck suppers in the church basement, known as the green rooms, not because they had anything in common with those used in theater and television, but because the walls were tiled in light green ceramic tile. Some of the moms were part of our parish's chapter of the "Legion of Decency," which rated movies and books for their suitability for Catholics. The ratings were found in *The*

New World, a Catholic newspaper published by the Archdiocese of Chicago, and copied into *The St. Felicitas News*, our weekly church bulletin. Before we could go to a movie, we had to make sure the listing said it was an "A" movie. There were degrees of A-ness, 1, 2, 3, because we didn't have the G, PG, R ratings that help parents decide today. It was up to the Legion of Decency to keep us away from "B" movies. The "B" here didn't mean low-budget. It was much more risqué than that. Not that I ever saw one.

For the dads there was the Holy Name Society. I have no idea what they did, but that was how the dads knew each other. They missed most of our weekday activities at school; they had to work. My dad also played poker at the rectory, with the priests. I had the idea that there was whiskey involved, and cigars. I suppose other dads might have been there. I don't know if it was an official Holy Name Society function, but it is what I remember the most. Moms and dads both served as scout leaders and the athletic dads coached our sports teams. Mine was not one of those.

The parish fish fries, on Fridays in Lent, were organized by the Boy Scouts and held in the school basement. They would set up long folding tables and a buffet line with fried perch, a nice Midwestern fish. We only had frozen fish sticks at my house, so this was a step up for me. Parents were there, and kids were there, and kids would be running around. It was a fun time for us; you could be a kid and just let loose. I vividly recall choking on a bone from one of those perch. It shocked me, since I'd never eaten fresh fish before, but I knew, with all those dads in attendance, I would be saved. And I was.

Laura's mother was a schoolteacher, so she needed a babysitter during the day for her younger children. Laura shared this memory with me:

> "I remember one time we were going to a babysitter's house. I was in the car and I looked out and there was a play area at an apartment building, and there was a black girl and a white girl playing together. I had never seen that before. We were all

white then in our school and neighborhood. I was watching them and said, 'Mom, look at . . .' I might have said the word colored, I don't know, 'that colored girl and white girl are playing together.' And she said to me, 'Well, you'll do that someday, too.' And I remember thinking, 'That's nice.' It just struck me that I had never seen a black child and white child playing together. There was nothing negative about it. It was just something unusual that I wondered about."

That's Life in the Big City

Chicago is a big city. There was danger there long before the racial unrest began in my neighborhood. The feeling of safety and security we felt was not really the same as what I imagine was experienced by someone growing up in a small town somewhere farther south, Mayberry, for instance. There were rules we were to follow, and we knew they were for our own good. We locked our homes and our car doors and had to be in the house by the time the street lights came on. There were busy streets with lots of traffic in between my house and those of my friends. There were rules about which streets you could cross that changed as you got older. I don't remember there being any talk about specific dangers, no "stranger danger" lectures in those years. But I tended to be cautious by nature—or maybe it was by nurture?

My friend Eileen is still haunted by something that happened to her when we were very young. She was with another girl who was a couple of years older when they were approached by some teenage boys on bikes. There were some houses on her block that were still being built. For some reason they were not locked. A boy whistled from the window of one of the houses, letting the boys on bikes know he was inside. The boys took Eileen and her friend into the house. She never found out what happened to her friend; that family moved away soon after. Eileen was taken by one of the boys into the basement. She remembers a second boy coming down the stairs, saying, "What are you doing?" She doesn't have a clear memory of what happened, but knows she told her parents. As she remembers it, our pastor, Monsignor Walsh, came to their house and asked them not to press charges. The boys were parishioners. Her parents did what Monsignor asked of them.

Something bad also happened to my sister and me when we were very small. Like Eileen, I was much older before I realized how badly this could have turned out. We were probably six and eight years old and not yet allowed to go very far from home. We were supposed to stay on our block, in fact. It was a big Chicago block with plenty of sidewalk for roller skating and lots of kids to play with, so that was not usually such a tough restriction. But just across 81st Street at the farthest point on the block from our house, was the public elementary school which had a playground—a much nicer playground than the one at our school—and it was *so close*. One day, we decided to throw caution to the wind and cross the street for just a short visit. I'm pretty sure this was my sister's idea; I was the naturally cautious one. But what harm could come from crossing one lousy street? Lots, as it turned out. I don't think what happened really had anything to do with us crossing the street, but it probably had everything to do with being at a playground alone. Before we even got to the gate to enter that forbidden paradise of swings and slides, a car pulled up at the curb. It was a unique car, not the only one of its kind, but one that I will never forget—two-tone, black and pink, with fins. Maybe it was the uniqueness of the car, or perhaps we were just obsessively polite children, but we approached it when the driver spoke to us. He was asking us directions. Imagine a thirty-something man in a nice car asking two small children at a playground for directions. Nothing about that sounds right, except to the children who were flattered this stranger would think we were a source of information. As we got close to the car, we noticed that he had something in his lap. We later told our parents it looked like a big thumb.

Luckily, we were really pretty timid children and did not often disobey our parents. We knew we were somewhere we were not supposed to be, so we certainly shouldn't be close to a

20

stranger's car there. He may have asked us to get in, but our radar told us to get home quickly; we did not hesitate to take off running home to tell our parents. I cannot imagine how our parents felt when we confessed our transgression. If we hadn't been so frightened, we would not have admitted we had broken such a big rule. We didn't get punished for it, but I also don't recall anyone making us feel that we had been in any serious danger. We just thought it was weird. The police came, though, so that was certainly something out of the ordinary. We were able to describe the man—I remember saying he had "sandy blond hair," which was probably how my mother described my hair. My sister remembers riding in a police car around the neighborhood, looking for the pink and black car. I was apparently considered too young to ride with the police. A few weeks later, though, we were both taken to the police station to identify a suspect—he had jet black hair. I overheard my mother on the phone with a friend soon after expressing how ridiculous it was that they had us come all the way to the police station when the person didn't even have the same hair color. Was that really all that bothered her about this event in my early life?

I don't know that they ever found the man. I do remember the moment in my twenties when I understood how much danger we might have been in. I appreciate that my parents, who must have been distraught, did not convey their fears to us. This could have haunted my childhood, but I didn't know then that it should.

My friend Laura told me a story about a man who scared her. I wonder now if it might have been the same guy. Her house was only three short blocks from that forbidden playground. Here is the story, in Laura's words:

> "The Harper flasher is vivid in my memory. We walked to school, about three blocks, usually in groups, but sometimes, as kids will do, there would be a couple in back, a couple in front. And I remember seeing the flasher on Harper Avenue one time, on the two long blocks between my house and the crossing guard. This time it was after school,

around 3:30. He was a white guy, looked like a regular dad, but he had the stereotypical overcoat on, and, as he approached children, he would just open up his overcoat. Flashers typically don't attack, but we didn't know that; we were all scared. It was the talk of the neighborhood. I don't think anyone called the police. Everybody just put up with it. He would show up, then he'd be gone, then he would show up, sporadically. Maybe he chose Harper because there were so many kids walking on that street. I think I just had a sense of safety, even with the flasher. I felt there were so many people in the neighborhood that would help you. You could walk up to anybody's house and knock on their door. Their mom would help you. I think that is why we felt so safe."

There was a beautiful old movie theater, The Avalon, on 79th Street, only a few blocks from my house. It opened in the twenties and was designed by a famous architect, John Eberson, who created many of the "movie palaces" of that era. I remember going there to see such classics as Mary Poppins and staring up at the ceiling which looked very much like the night sky. When we were little, one of our parents went with us, or my older sister might be in charge, but, at some point, I distinctly remember being dropped off to go in with just my sister Terry or a friend my age, with no adult supervision. Terry remembers being warned not to eat too much of the delicious buttered popcorn; I remember being told not, under any circumstances, to go into the restrooms. Apparently, danger lurked there. I never asked exactly what, but I never went in to find out, either.

There was also danger associated with our local YMCA. We went there to learn to swim, or at least to take swimming lessons. My mother was afraid of the water and passed that fear on to us, whether she meant to or not. But the water was not the only danger at the Y. Although it was just a few blocks from our house, it was in Chatham, the next neighborhood over. To get there you had to walk under a viaduct—a very large and dark overpass created by several elevated train tracks. I wasn't allowed to walk there alone. Chatham had become predominantly African American by this time. I don't remember any discussion about that, but I somehow had a sense that we weren't as safe there as we were in our neighborhood. Other than the Y, there was no reason for us to go there, and we didn't.

The Age of Reason

A major life event, for children who grow up Catholic, is First Holy Communion. For us, this happened in the spring of second grade; that entire school year was really just a big buildup to it. After Baptism, Communion, and its related sacrament, Confession, are the next up of the seven Catholic sacraments. Our religious instruction was stepped up a notch, so we would understand the significance of both of them. Communion is the main event in the mass, so it is a really big deal to be considered old enough to receive it.

Key to going to Communion was first confessing your sins to a priest, to make you worthy. Confession was very private back then. We stood in line outside the confessional until it was our turn to go in and kneel in the dark booth. The priest moved a window across a screen so that he could hear you. He had a booth on either side of him, so that he didn't lose any time while the people making their confessions, the penitents, were changing places. When you first knelt down, you could hear mumblings of the priest and the penitent on the other side, but you were not supposed to even attempt to listen. When the window opened, you couldn't see the priest, who was behind a screen, but we always knew their voices, and we sometimes watched to see which priest went into which booth (there were four in our church), as we had our favorites. Confession began with these exact words: "Bless me Father for I have sinned," then we were to say how long it had been since our last Confession. The first time we just said: "this is my first

Confession." You were to then confess the sins you had committed since your last Confession, which for your first Confession meant your entire seven-year life. I remember having to really think hard to come up with something to confess. I was a pretty good kid. I probably went with lying since even little white lies were to be confessed and maybe disrespecting someone, a teacher would do. When you got all that out, the priest would forgive you, contingent on your completing a penance that he came up with right on the spot. Penance for seven-year-olds usually consisted of reciting a couple of prayers, mostly Hail Marys and Our Fathers. Come to think of it, that is what penance was for as long as I went to confession, about eight years. It might have progressed to entire rosaries, which meant multiple Hail Marys and Our Fathers, but I don't remember ever having to actually *do* anything. But then again, my sins stayed pretty consistently boring, too. It seems absurd to me now that second graders were being taught that they were sinners in need of absolution, but it felt like quite a privilege to me then. At seven we had reached what we were told was the "age of reason," a time when we could no longer claim we didn't know the difference between right and wrong. Confession always felt uncomfortable to me, but it was the price you had to pay if you wanted to participate in the ritual of Communion—beginning with the biggest day of our lives up until that point—the First Communion day itself.

On the designated Sunday morning in April, we second-grade girls paraded into the church, wearing frilly white dresses and veils, side by side with boys in dress shirts and ties, ready to partake in the sacrament for the first time. We had not only been prepared religiously, we had rehearsed the walk into the church and up to the altar rail for weeks, if not months, so that it would all be perfect on the big day. I remember feeling very grown up and extremely holy—and a bit like a fairy princess in my dress and veil, hand-me-downs from my sisters, but still quite beautiful. Everyone's parents and siblings were there, smiling and taking photos, and the whole parish was watching. Afterward, there was an actual grown-up party at our house in my honor. My godfather was there, probably the only time he'd been at our house since my Baptism, along with my parents' closest friends and their children. My friends couldn't be there because they were being feted at their own homes at the same time—except for Sheila, who had the measles. Her parents took her to the church after we were all gone to take photos, but she didn't get to walk with us, and I doubt they had a party. (Measles was a really big problem, it was highly contagious, and the first vaccine wasn't released until the following year.) At my party there was ham, and potato salad, and probably a cake. I don't think there were presents involved, but I did get some mementos of the big day that I still have—a statue of a young girl being given communion by Jesus and a small prayer book with an angel on the shiny, cardboard cover. Once the day itself had passed, we were allowed to join in communion every day before school and, even better, we got to go to the bakery for that donut breakfast in its little white paper bag.

The Luck of the Irish

When someone asks me my ethnicity, I often respond by saying that I was "raised Irish Catholic." In Chicago this combination of nationality and religion carries a very specific connotation. But the Heppners are not really the least bit Irish. My dad's mother's family came from Germany in the mid-1800s, settling in the farm country of Indiana. His father came over as a young man near the end of the 1890s, from a part of Germany that is now part of Poland. They settled near the steel mills on the southeast side of Chicago, not far from St. Felicitas, although our parish didn't exist back then. My mother's family can be traced back many generations in the U.S., then to England. I didn't know any of this back in elementary school, though.

I remember one time in about the third grade when I was supposed to find out what nationality I was and report it at school the next day. Running out to be on time to mass one morning, I asked my mom what we were. Her quick, on her feet, answer was "German, Dutch and Irish." Mom claimed later she thought the Broadheads (her father's family) were Irish, but it is an English name and England and Ireland, although geographically close, are definitely not the same. My ancestry searches over the years have not turned up anyone from Ireland. I believe now that she threw in the Irish that day because she knew it was important to be Irish, at least a little bit Irish, at St. Felicitas. After all, our pastor was Monsignor Walsh and he was assisted by Fathers O'Donnell and Kelley.

Thousands of European immigrants settled on the South Side of Chicago around the turn of the twentieth century. As immigrants are prone to do, people from the same country, even the same village, settled near one another, where there were people they knew and who understood their language. The Catholic parishes in each of these ethnic neighborhoods tended to reflect the single nationality that dominated their neighborhood. I don't know if the Polish parish or the Italian parish had priests that actually *were* Polish or Italian, but we knew which parishes were which, and they knew we were an Irish parish. We certainly weren't the only Irish parish, given the number of Irish that settled in Chicago.

St. Patrick's Day was a very big deal at St. Felicitas, especially to Father Kelley. We had a St. Patty's Day school program every year, specifically for his benefit. He visited every classroom on the big day so that we could sing "Has Anybody Here Seen Kelly," for him. He always had a cigar in his mouth, although I never saw it lit, and he brought us all tokens, which I assumed were from Ireland. I remember one year he gave us all little green toy frogs. I always thought there was some relationship between frogs and Ireland, but I guess they were just green. And fun. My frog was only about two inches long, made of metal with a spring on the bottom that could be set by squishing it into a little bit of putty that was stuck there. As the putty lost its grip, the frog would hop! This was quite big stuff, in that era, before plastic and battery-powered toys.

At most of our school programs there was Irish music played, and sometimes kids would do Irish dances. One particular family had several girls who could dance jigs and had cool costumes, traditional Irish dresses with lots of ribbons. No one ever tried to teach the rest of us to do the dances, so I thought it was genetic. You had to be really, really, Irish, not just a quarter, to dance like that. I can't be sure, since I never attended the other churches in the city, but my guess is that our version of religious ceremonies had a little bit of an Irish twist, too.

I remember being mesmerized when one of our nuns read us a chapter a day from "The Babe Ruth Story." I would have sworn he was Irish. He was actually German, but the nun didn't mention that. He was Catholic, and he grew up in a Catholic reform school, which is also where he learned to play baseball.

Irish Americans and Catholics had a hero in the early sixties in John Fitzgerald Kennedy, an Irish Catholic from Massachusetts, elected our first (and still only) Catholic President on November 8, 1960. I was in the first grade and just learning to read, but I was aware that there was an election and decided I would support Richard Nixon. I shared my decision with my father, who found it quite humorous. I have no idea who he supported; my parents believed in the privacy of the ballot box and never told us who they voted for. Reflecting on this now, I wonder if I was just trying to be contrary, as I would imagine any messages I was getting at St. Felicitas were firmly in support of the Catholic candidate.

My friend Eileen had an Italian father and an Italian last name. She was half Irish but always wished she was all Irish and had an Irish name. She remembers the nuns saying that a marriage between Irish and Italian would be bad because both have fiery tempers. Eileen took some offense at this; it did not describe her parents. Sheila's father was Irish, but he was the "Orange" (protestant) kind, not the favored "Green" (Catholic) variety. She also took offense when, in the third grade, our nuns told us such "mixed" marriages were risky because the non-Catholic parent, who would have had to agree to raise the children Catholic, might change his mind and expose the kids to Protestantism. Sheila's never did.

It's interesting that the nuns decided to talk to us about marriage in the third grade, but we didn't find it unusual at the time. I have a vivid memory of standing up to share my bright idea for ensuring the compatibility of the couple—live together before getting married. I thought I was the first person to think this up. The nuns were not amused. But they had some bright ideas of their own. For example, to encourage us to respect our mothers, they would tell us of children who went off to school in the morning after being mean to their mothers, and, when they came home that afternoon, their mother was dead. When one of our classmates died, I distinctly remember the nun telling us that the poor girl got an infection in her brain from wiping her nose without a handkerchief. Although I don't recall being told the fabled "black patent leather shoes reflect up" story, I do remember learning that divorce was caused by wives wearing dirty white tennis shoes. Guess that was part of the marriage lecture for ten-year-old girls, too.

The Garage is on Fire! Really, the Garage was on Fire

Our family was not opposed to spending time in front of the television. My parents hadn't grown up with TV and didn't get their first set until my oldest sister was five or six, but I don't remember a time without it. After dinner, my dad would usually have to go to his desk in the basement to do "bookwork" for his grocery store, and my mom had to clean up the kitchen; I was never asked to help either one of them. My sister Connie might have homework from high school, but my sister Terry and I moved right to the living room to watch television. One night after the dishes were done and my dad had finished his bookwork, the four of us were watching some sitcom or another, probably "My Three Sons." Connie was not home; it must have been a Friday night. Suddenly, we heard sirens, which kept getting louder and louder. We looked out our front window and saw smoke about a block away. Then we heard a horrible noise, it sounded like multiple air horns being blown at once. My dad said it was a car horn and its continual blaring must mean the car was on fire. My mom immediately started to fret that it might be her beloved car—a 1962 Cadillac, complete with fins. My parents were products of The Great Depression; they did not spend money needlessly, but my dad really loved nice cars. Each of my parents had a car, but our house only had a one-car garage. It wasn't big enough for the Cadillac, so my mom rented a garage from a neighbor. The sirens, flashing lights, and smoke were all coming from the block where her car had been safely stored that afternoon. Mom was sure she recognized the sound of her Cadillac's horn. The noise went on for a while; the firemen were now at work, but just out of our sight. Then we heard the same screeching coming from the other direction. My dad wouldn't let us go outside, so we didn't know until morning that three nearby garages and the cars inside them were destroyed by fire that night. Luckily, my mom's car was not one of them. One of the cars did turn out to be a Cadillac, though. Maybe their horn sound really was unique.

The whole neighborhood seemed to be outside the next day. My mom let me walk with her to see the two garages that were within a couple blocks of our house. The smell of burned-out buildings is something I will never forget. Sort of like the remnants of a log fire in the fireplace, but with a whiff of chemicals, probably from the gasoline. The buildings were also wet, having been doused by the firemen's hoses the night before, which added a musty smell. I don't know if anyone ever found out who set the fires. At that age the whole episode faded quickly from my memory, but I'm sure my parents did not forget.

Our neighbors across the street moved away about this time. I don't know why they moved, but my parents missed them, they were both neighbors and friends. One afternoon, I heard yelling on the street between our homes and looked out the window in time to see a group of white teenage boys I didn't know riding by on their bikes. They were shouting something I couldn't make out and throwing stones at our new neighbor's house. The family that had moved in was white, but apparently the kids didn't know that.

Our sense of safety was starting to give way; our neighborhood was gradually changing. As a country, the post-war time of relative peace ended abruptly with the Cuban Missile Crisis in October of 1962. I remember lying in bed in the room I shared with my sister and listening to an old radio. I don't recall exactly what we were listening to and would have been too young to comprehend what was happening, but I knew that everyone was afraid, and it was something big. Like many of the events of my childhood, it was many years before I would learn the reality of this event and recognize the fear that my parents must have felt.

There Goes the Parish

While I was still in my early years at St. Felicitas, black families had begun to move into our neighborhood. Some of my friends remember hearing that our pastor, Monsignor Walsh, had tried to reassure his parishioners, telling them that, if they didn't panic, the neighborhood would be "stable." If he could keep families from moving out in large numbers, the typical pattern of white flight, he seemed to feel things could go on as usual. I don't know how he defined "stable," but his words would certainly be viewed as racist today. He wasn't openly resisting blacks moving in, though, just the mass exodus of whites that had occurred in other neighborhoods. He probably also wanted to keep enough parishioners to support the parish church and school. There was no guarantee the new property owners would be Catholic or send their children to parochial schools.

My sister Connie hung on to some parish bulletins from this time. Our weekly bulletin, creatively named "The St. Felicitas News," was a five-by-six-inch newsletter, handed out at Sunday mass. I imagine it was written by Monsignor Walsh, or at least approved by him before it was printed. Below is an excerpt from Sunday, June 3, 1962. The first sections of that edition were typical parish announcements with these headings: List of High Masses, Your Prayers, Please!, Baptisms, Novena Devotions, Vigil of the Pentecost, Holy Name Society, Promises of Marriage, Altar and Rosary Society—then this:

SOUTH AVALON COMMUNITY ORGANIZATION

The South Avalon Community Organization will hold an important and general meeting in the Green Rooms on next Wednesday Night at 8 o'clock. There will be election of Officers and Board members. An interesting program has been arranged. All residents of South Avalon should be present. We congratulate South Avalon on its very successful membership drive last Sunday. More than sixty new members have been added. The people of South Avalon are determined to keep and improve their Community. They fear nothing and will combat block busters, avaricious realtors, false rumors, and violators of the Building Code. Your help is needed. It is your civic duty to attend this meeting.

SECO

The South East Community Organization is determined to keep our Community, Marynook, North Avalon, South Avalon, and East of Stony Island Avenue, stable. Its various Committees on Building Code, Public Information, Law Enforcement, Real Estate are working hard and will produce splendid results. There is no need for panic or hysteria. Many homes in our Community are being sold to new parishioners of Saint Felicitas Parish. The best salesmen of our fine residential area must be its confident residents. St. Felicitas is the Patron of our Parish and we have put her in charge of the Community. St. Felicitas and her seven sons will not let us down. And neither should you. We place everything in the hands of God with St.

Felicitas and her Seven Sons "packing a big wallop."

Then back to normal business, with sections titled Legion of Decency, Apartments for Rent and Our Softball League, followed by four advertisements, two for funeral homes.

My sister also kept an edition of the St. Felicitas News from the next month, which again included apartments for rent in the parish. Both newsletters include the same woman's name and phone number to contact for the rentals. In the July edition, there is also a section titled "FOR SALE," with three homes listed, all very close to the church. Connie, who was in high school at the time, remembers hearing that the parish was buying homes to ensure they would be sold, or rented, to people who would join the parish. Catholics. Maybe white Catholics?

The two organizations listed in The St. Felicitas News remind me of the seminal 1959 Broadway play, "A Raisin in the Sun," written by Lorraine Hansberry and based partly on her family's experience in Chicago. In the play, a representative of the Clybourne Park Improvement Association, ostensibly representing its "welcoming committee," pays a visit to the black family at the center of the plot, that has just purchased a home in the fictional all-white Clybourne Park neighborhood. The representative who, of course, is a white man, offers to buy the home at a profit to the black family, explaining to them that the people of Clybourne Park feel "our Negro families are happier when they live in their *own* communities," while at the same time assuring them that "race prejudice simply doesn't enter into it."[1] This example is clearly racist, while our church newsletter only hints at the underlying reason that the South Avalon Community Organization and SECO were taking up the cause of keeping our neighborhood "stable."

My sister Terry remembers being treated oddly by a nun around this time. She thinks it was because my father had taken a stand against what he felt were blatant attempts by the parish to keep blacks out of the neighborhood. Dad told her years later that there was a specific house just about a block from ours that the church purchased because they did not want it to be bought by blacks. The block had several parish families living there, and there were many, many young white children who played on that street. Terry also remembers a day when Dad was going to drive us somewhere, he picked us up on the corner in front of our house, instead of our usual place next to the garage. She heard later that someone had written "n****r lover" on our garage door. I have no memory of this; I was only about eight, so oblivious to most everything outside of my personal space.

Meanwhile, Back at School

None of this changed what was about to happen inside good old St. Felicitas grammar school. I recall Paula Wilson as the first African-American student in my class. She arrived at the beginning of fifth grade. I don't remember her being introduced or anything special about her being there. She probably just started that school year with us. I suppose we had new kids every year, but I don't really remember that. We weren't with the same kids every year. We had two classrooms, sometimes two and a half or three for each grade, with between 40 and 50 kids in a room, so you didn't always have the same group. After what seemed to us to be really, really, long summer vacations, you might not remember anyone from the prior school year. Paula was tall, had a dark brown complexion, and wore her hair in braids, so she stood out. Nobody made a big deal about it; it was just unusual enough to be memorable.

As it turns out, the first African Americans actually joined our grade two years before, in the third grade, but they weren't in my room. Our memories during those early years are pretty specific to what happened in the room we were assigned. We didn't change classes; we spent all day in "our" room. My friend Beth showed me her third-grade class photo; it includes two black students, one boy and one girl. Beth remembers them being introduced to the class. The teacher made a point of telling the children to make sure these newcomers felt welcome. Beth recalled that all the girls wanted to be this new little girl's friend. Laura was also in that classroom and remembers that the new girl was very cute, and Laura hoped they would be seated next to each other. There were no negative feelings, but, like my first memory of Paula, this "new girl" was notable enough to be recalled easily fifty years later.

Chapter 2

TWEENS

In the "middle" grades—fourth, fifth, sixth—a few more African-American students joined our class each year. It seemed normal to us kids, although we did not mingle with them in quite the same way we did with the white kids. I asked my friends if the nuns at our school treated the black students any differently than they treated the white students. They all said no; they felt the nuns went out of their way to treat everyone the same, or even to treat the black students favorably, to be sure they felt welcome.

Kathy Richards is the first black girl Sheila remembers. They were probably in the same room, but Sheila says she remembers her because they were "best buddies." Kathy lived in Marynook, right on Sheila's route to school. Sheila spent time in Kathy's home and considers her a good friend from childhood who she lost touch with over the years. When I reconnected with Kathy as an adult, she reminded me that she skipped eighth grade to start high school early. That is probably why we lost touch with her. I found it interesting that anyone would opt out of eighth grade, that year full of rituals and celebrations that the rest of us felt would be the pinnacle of our childhood. Maybe St. Felicitas was not as much fun for Kathy as it was for me.

Beth remembers being invited to a birthday party at Karen Jones's house in the fourth grade. Apparently, other white girls were invited, although I don't remember being one of them. I probably wasn't in her room that year. Beth's father would not let her go. Beth thinks her mother probably would have let her go, but her father said, "No, I don't want you over there." Karen lived in our neighborhood, so it wasn't that he didn't want her to go to a certain part of town; he just didn't want her in the home of an African-American family. He didn't have to give her a reason. Our dads didn't justify their decisions to their children.

At this point we were still living in our cocoon of safety while, in June of 1963, Alabama governor George Wallace was physically blocking the doors to the University of Alabama so that black students could not enter. That summer The Reverend Dr. Martin Luther King, Jr. delivered his historic "I Have a Dream" speech at the March on Washington and, in September, a church in Birmingham, Alabama was bombed, killing four young girls about my age. These events were no doubt on the front page of the newspaper in Chicago, which my mother read every morning, but I didn't know about any of them until I was an adult.

Kennedy Assassination

Our wider world, the one that contained our beloved Irish Catholic President, was again proven unsafe two months later. Although I was a healthy child and don't remember missing much school, I was home sick from fourth grade on November 22, 1963. My sister had already come home for lunch and headed back to school. My mother was outside talking to our neighbor, Mrs. Cooper, over the back fence. I was in the living room watching Bozo's Circus on television. The last thing that always happened on Bozo's Circus was the "grand prize game," which involved kids throwing something into buckets that were in a row in front of them. The kid who got the object into the farthest bucket was the winner. Just at the most suspenseful moment, when the last objects would be tossed to determine who would win that day's competition, the news broke in to tell me that President Kennedy had been shot in Dallas. I ran outside to tell my mother, then returned to find out who won the grand prize game. I never found out. The news didn't leave the television for the next three days—and neither did we.

About an hour after the first announcement of the shooting, my mother and I got the bad news that the President was dead. My friends at school heard both these announcements over the intercom

36

from Sister Thea, our principal, who was undoubtedly choking back tears. Schools closed early that day, but I don't recall my sisters coming home. I don't remember my father coming home from work that day either, but I know for sure we were all gathered around the television when Jack Ruby shot Lee Harvey Oswald that Saturday. We watched JFK's funeral procession and saw the salute that little John John gave his father. I've seen many documentaries about those events over the years that attempt to recreate the drama, but those of us who lived it will never forget how surreal it was, watching it unfold live on the television in our living rooms with our families around us. I was nine years old and can remember it like it was yesterday. I felt a profound sense of sadness and loss, along with disbelief, that was only made worse by knowing that my parents felt it, too.

Other Milestones

Lyndon Baines Johnson, LBJ, who I had never heard of, became President, and fourth grade continued. For my class that meant preparing for another Catholic ritual, Confirmation, to be held in the spring. This time we were not only of the age of reason, we were old enough to personally "confirm" our loyalty to the church. At least I think that is what it was all about. It certainly wasn't optional, not at St. Felicitas School anyway. There were no pretty dresses involved, we wore our everyday uniforms, but they were pretty new then and we did clean and press them for the occasion. Some of us were considered grown up enough to wear nylons, too. Nylons are what we called the predecessor to pantyhose. We were still wearing chapel veils on our heads in church that year; for confirmation we wore red ones. I don't remember if that had something to do with our school colors, or if red was considered somehow sacred. To be confirmed required someone of a higher rank than the priests in our church, generally a bishop. Our class was honored to be confirmed by "His Eminence Cardinal Meyer," as I was reminded by my sloppy fourth-grade handwriting on the back of a holy card I kept as a memento of the occasion. Having the Cardinal was a really big deal.

The spring of 1964 is also known for the "Beatles Invasion." I was still very young when we first heard of the Beatles, but my older sisters loved popular music, so I knew the latest hits. Our family gathered around the TV together again the night that the Beatles were on Ed Sullivan.

That summer, President Johnson would sign the most significant piece of legislation of the era, The Civil Rights Act of 1964, barring discrimination on the basis of race. But the Civil Rights Movement was far from over. In March of 1965, The Reverend Dr. Martin Luther King, Jr. led thousands on an historic walk from Selma to Montgomery to support voting rights for blacks. The Voting Rights Act was passed the next year; less than a week later there were riots, also historic, in the Watts area of Los Angeles.

My time in fifth and sixth grade included a massive buildup of American troops in Vietnam, doubling from 200,000 to 400,000 between 1965 and 1966. Daily counts of casualties became routine on the evening news. But we kids were mostly oblivious to the larger world events that would shape our generation. Things were still relatively safe in our neighborhood, but we were hit hard when we lost a classmate to leukemia in January of 1965. I'll never forget her wake and funeral. They buried her in her St. Felicitas school uniform.

Avalon Park

Once we got into the double digits—10, 11, 12—we were allowed to go to the park with our friends. We already knew the park from trips there with our parents earlier; it was a big part of our lives and our neighborhood. Avalon Park is still one of the most beautiful properties of the Chicago Park District. Opened in the 1930s, it includes nearly 28 acres of green space and a field house which was brand new when I was four. The park faces 83rd Street, only a few blocks from St. Felicitas. I lived closer to the park than

I did to my school. The west side of the park is bordered by the Illinois Central Railroad—our access to downtown Chicago—which also serves as the western boundary of our neighborhood and parish. The other two sides of the park border the part of our neighborhood known as Marynook.

Kids played softball at the park and, in the summer, romped around in the 1960s version of a splash pad, a shallow concrete pool with one big water spray, a step up from the fire hydrants. People picnicked there and our school football team practiced and played their home games there. The park's field house has a gym where we learned to play bombardment and watched boys play basketball. The field house is also where I remember learning to sew. In winter, an open field in the park was flooded to create an ice-skating rink. I liked ice skating so much I took lessons, dreaming of the Olympics, no doubt; it was the time of Peggy Fleming. Starting in about fifth grade, I had free reign to go to the park with my friends, no parental supervision required. We really had a great deal of independence and would walk or ride our bikes throughout the neighborhood, often into the park. Avalon Park was a tremendous community asset and a central theme in our childhood.

Eileen's father coached little league baseball at the park. Hundreds of boys from our neighborhood played on little league teams. One time, when Eileen and I were in about fifth grade, her dad and his team were there practicing when some black kids came up and took the bike of one of his players. All the kids' bikes were there while they practiced; bikes were our primary form of transportation. There were probably twenty boys as well as coaches involved in the baseball practice, and these kids no one knew had the nerve to take a bike right in front of them. The players tried to go after the bike thieves, but Eileen's father stopped them. He followed the thieves himself, thinking he could retrieve the bike and hopefully scare them into realizing what they had done was wrong. Kids were supposed to fear the wrath of parents and other adults, right? The police came and arrested him, Eileen's dad, for "inciting a riot." Her dad's nickname was "Honest Mike." Inciting a riot is the last thing he would ever do. He was stopping his ball players, who wanted to find the thieves and start a fight. He was hoping to teach the young bike thieves a lesson, as he would his own kids and those he coached, yet he was the one arrested. Our world was starting to make less and less sense.

The girls also played sports at Avalon Park, although there were no organized leagues for us. One time in sixth grade, a few of my girlfriends were at the park playing softball after school when they spotted a group of black kids approaching them. The group, which included both boys and girls, seemed to target my friends, following them as they tried to leave the park. The girls got frightened and ran toward a house near the park where the family of one of our classmates lived. It was a big family, so someone was usually at home. The black kids escalated from just following them to throwing things at them and hitting them on their backs and pulling their hair, until the girls finally reached the safety of the home of someone they knew and trusted.

The next day, Laura told our sixth-grade teacher, a nun, about the incident. One of the black kids involved was a student at our school. Laura told the nun that she and her friends were minding their own business, playing a game, when they were attacked for no reason. The nun reacted with anger towards Laura, saying she didn't understand what black people had to deal with and telling her she was behaving like a spoiled child. Laura still remembers feeling betrayed; she felt what happened was unjust. She and her friends didn't provoke it, so she thought her teacher would support her and say the other kids were in the wrong, punish them. Instead, she and her friends were made to feel they were guilty of something and they deserved what happened to them.

One quadrant of our parish, the one that bordered the park, was an area named Marynook. Everyone knew it was called that because there was a giant sign right at the corner of Dorchester and 83rd Street. Giant as in four feet high and fifteen feet long, as I remember it. I have a vague memory of walking to see the exciting new Marynook development with my mother and some other adults when it was just being built. That big sign was only a block from our house. This memory is fuzzy because I couldn't have been more than three or four years old. Some older St. Felicitas alumni remember catching frogs and tadpoles in the swamp that was on that site before the homes were built. Chicago Magazine has described Marynook as "a developer's late-1950s attempt at keeping city residents from fleeing to the suburbs." I guess it makes sense to compare it to a suburb, since the houses were all new in the fifties and the area has curved streets that are not seen anywhere else nearby. It certainly looked different from the houses on my street—all 1920s era brick bungalows laid out on a grid system. But I didn't know what a suburb was back then, and I certainly hadn't heard about anyone fleeing to them. Several of my classmates, including Eileen and Sheila, lived in Marynook, so I had lots of opportunity to be in the homes there over the years. Those houses were nothing like ours on the inside either. They were split level, which made them seem really small, each floor was only one or two rooms. They were definitely cute, though. If you have seen the movie "Edward Scissorhands," you have a pretty good idea what Marynook looked like when it was new.

One of the nice features of Marynook is that it has pedestrian walkways that take you right from some of its streets into Avalon Park. I imagine the proximity of the park played into the decision of the developer to create Marynook there. The park pathways were narrow, with tall bushes on either side. Once you were a few feet onto the path you couldn't see the street and you couldn't be seen by people walking or driving in the neighborhood. The bushes were also thick enough that you couldn't see into the yards you were passing and the people in the yards couldn't see you. These were easy places for kids to hide and scare one another. In the mid-sixties, for me and my girlfriends, that meant black kids hiding and jumping out at unsuspecting white kids. Those walkways, and other quiet streets in Marynook, were the first places many of us remember being afraid of groups of black kids who, we learned, wanted to scare us or even hurt us, for reasons we didn't understand. I'm not sure they understood, either; we were all just kids.

Eileen's house was on the outer edge of Marynook, so her

41

quickest way home from the park was to use one of the walkways through the bushes, then walk through the back section of Marynook. One day in sixth grade, as she was entering the street from the park pathway, a group of black youths started following her. She started walking faster; they started running, so she started running. She had to cut through the yard behind her house and jump the fence to get home, but they didn't catch her. They succeeded in scaring her, though.

Laura also remembers a day about this time when she was walking home alone from the park. She saw a group of black kids and got scared because she had heard stories from her friends about being chased and beaten up, what we called getting "jumped." The kids started taunting her, saying things like, "Hey, white girl," and cat-calling "whitey" at her. She got scared, not knowing what might happen. She still remembers her heart rate getting high as she started to walk faster, eventually running home, although the kids didn't give chase.

As the stories of these events were spread, among both the neighborhood kids and our parents, eventually they could not be ignored or trivialized. Each time something happened, we knew that one day we would not be allowed to go to our wonderful park. That was how it always turned out. We did nothing wrong and yet we suffered the consequences by losing a privilege. Eventually, by the start of eighth grade, my friends and I, the girls, at least, were not allowed to go to the park alone because of our parents' fear that we would get hurt by these groups of black youths. I don't know if the park managers or the police talked to the kids who perpetrated the acts, punishing or at least reprimanding them, but we were being punished. It made us feel victimized, not just by the kids who chased us, but by the adults who controlled our world at the time.

Race Relations

Within St. Felicitas School things continued to be quite peaceful. A few more African-American students joined us in the sixth grade. Laura remembers Denise Albert, who was pale but not quite the same shade of white as the rest of us. She seemed quite unusual; her family was from Haiti and she spoke with an accent. I imagine that we were pretty unusual to her, too. The teacher had her sit next to Laura and asked Laura to help her learn the ropes. Laura felt very flattered to be asked. I remember Denise because she walked home from school the same way I did at lunch. We often walked together, and I enjoyed her company. Like other childhood habits, this changed at some point; no particular reason, I just didn't happen to walk with her later on.

Laura also reminded me of an African-American girl who joined our class that year who had light, not quite white, blotches on her face. We both think now it was the disease that Michael Jackson had, vitiligo. I remember wondering as a kid if she had one white parent—we were really naïve and had no idea that it might be caused by a skin condition. I also remember the black woman who lived next door to us sunbathing in her back yard. We didn't get that at all. She was already the beautiful bronze color we were all hoping to get to when we sunbathed.

Beth was good friends with Linda Morgan, who was African American, and remembers the two of them getting into a fight with another girl who was also black. She doesn't remember what the fight was about but says it had nothing to do with race. Beth remembers the other girl as "tough," though, and I don't know that we used "tough" to describe any of our white classmates. Beth says the spat was just "girl witchy-ness." We were preteens at this point and being mean to other girls was not above any of us. The girl Beth and Linda were fighting with was Donna Jo Thompson. Beth had heard that her brothers were in gangs. One day later on, when Beth was in the park, Donna Jo's younger brother was there and threatened her, saying, "I want to beat you up and finish what my sister started."

Beth doesn't remember ever going to Linda's home, the way she often went to homes of her white friends. They were just "school friends." They didn't live near one another, which made it less likely they would visit each other's houses after school. We were still pretty young and not allowed to wander the entire neighborhood. Beth doesn't remember how they became friends, but assumes they sat near each other in class. Who you sat by made a difference in those classrooms packed with kids, all sitting in straight rows. We had assigned seats, generally based on height.

As more and more African Americans joined us at school, white families were moving out and we were losing friends each year. We didn't connect these two changes in our world to one another yet, so didn't begrudge the newcomers for the loss of our friends, or vice versa. With the increasing danger in the neighborhood, though, we became a little more cautious about befriending the new kids in our school. We were still friends with the black kids that moved in during third, fourth and fifth grade, in particular, but some of the newer arrivals were not as friendly to us, nor were we to them. We did connect the danger in the neighborhood to the racial change; it would have been hard not to, given that the stories we heard were all about black kids attacking white kids. It no longer felt like they wanted to be our friends. We started to wonder if they just wanted to push us all out.

Laura remembers a restaurant on 87th Street where she saw an interracial couple. Her mother pointed them out to her and told her that there were only a few restaurants in the whole city where white women dating black men could dine together and not be harassed. Laura also remembers an occasion when some of her aunts and uncles came to visit from a small community downstate. They told Laura's parents they thought they should leave the neighborhood; that they better get out because it was "changing." But her parents never said things like that, nor did mine. Our parents didn't really say much about the changing demographics, at least not to us. We all just accepted it at first, before kids started getting beaten up. Even then, we considered that to be the exception, since the black kids in our school were nice kids, and we mostly got along fine.

In 1966, The Reverend Dr. Martin Luther King, Jr. moved to Chicago. His home was in the West Side neighborhood of Lawndale. He lived there as part of The Chicago Freedom Movement, protesting housing conditions for blacks in the city.

Despite the gradual integration of neighborhoods like ours, most blacks in Chicago were still confined to substandard housing in what was known as the "Black Belt." Reverend King did not get a warm welcome from the city's leaders and he was not successful in Chicago. He was physically attacked during a nonviolent protest. In the end, he suggested that "people from Mississippi ought to come to Chicago to learn how to hate."[2, 3]

Traditions Continue

The traditions within St. Felicitas parish were continuing as usual. I remember Easter Sunday mass, primarily because the church was full of beautiful Easter lilies, after having been shrouded in purple cloth for all the weeks of Lent. But the most special mass to us was Midnight Mass. The idea was to celebrate the first moment, after midnight, of Christmas, the birthday of Jesus. As a kid, I assumed he had been born at midnight; I had been born just after midnight on my birthday. I don't think we actually waited until midnight to start the festivities, but it was definitely late, and it was the only time we were inside the church at night. The altar was decorated with poinsettias and real evergreen trees – and candles. There were always candles in our church, but at night they added a touch of elegance, even mystery to the mood of the church. There was a nativity scene, a large one, at the front of the church. No live animals, but very lifelike statues. We didn't have a choir at our church normally, everyone just sang along. It wasn't always the most melodic of sounds; during the time of the Latin mass I don't think it was meant to sound particularly joyous, more of a dirge. But at Midnight Mass the girls from the seventh and eighth grades came marching in singing and holding, not candles (too dangerous), but flashlights covered with red cellophane. It was magical, especially when you were one of those 100 or so girls. It felt great just to be in the church, to be a part of all that majesty.

A tradition that involved the entire community was the May Procession. May Processions, sometimes called May Crownings, were quite common in the sixties and are still held in some places

45

today. The Catholic Church honors Mary, the mother of Jesus, at all times, but celebrates her more openly during the month of May, often by crowning her queen of heaven after a procession in her honor. Our May Procession involved the entire enrollment of St. Felicitas School, close to a thousand kids some years, walking several blocks in a circuit around the neighborhood, starting on the playground and ending back on the same block, in the church. Several city streets were closed for the occasion. All of the parishioners, as well as many of our non-Catholic neighbors came out to watch; we were hard to miss. The atmosphere was both holy and festive. Each class of St. Felicitas walked with their classmates, in nice even rows, as was our norm. The second-grade girls got to wear their First Communion dresses again, and a few of the eighth-grade girls got to dress up in formal attire. The rest of the eighth graders got to wear their graduation ribbons, two ten-inch ribbons in the school colors embossed with the school name and their class year. The other students wore their uniforms, unless you had a special role to play. I wore my Girl Scout uniform one year and walked with my scout troupe. Our band had its own, very professional-looking, uniforms and accompanied us as we marched. The procession was led by none other than Monsignor Walsh himself, along with our other parish priests and a few altar boys—all in their religious attire and carrying the crucifix that would lead us into church—for a mass, of course. Like our other traditions, this one required numerous rehearsals. The neighborhood never felt safer than when we were rehearsing for the May Procession.

Inside the school things continued to have that safe and protected feeling, too. We sometimes feared the nuns but somehow knew they had our best interest in mind, even when they were threatening us. Our class sizes were still large, so the teachers had to be strict; they were badly outnumbered. Many of the stories my classmates remember from this era have to do with things we did when we thought the nuns couldn't see (or hear) us and the consequences when they did. Here are a few they shared for our fiftieth reunion:

- Winning a penmanship medal while I was chewing gum, then having to accept the award with the gum on the tip of my nose.
- One particularly mischievous boy jumping out a second-floor window during a bad snowstorm. *MIKE HINZ*
- Cooling off at the fire hydrant on a hot afternoon. Someone would get hold of a large wrench and bring it to the playground and the fun would begin. *MIKE AGAIN*
- Nuns putting kids out in "the oven" as punishment for misbehavior. (The oven was the tar roof outside one of the classrooms; it got hot out there!) *MIKE NOT BAD YET!*
- Sister Blanche yelling "MARCH" to anyone caught doing something against the rules. You then had to place a check mark next to your name on a posted list in the rear of the classroom.

SKIP JOE BURKE

And this one from a very special friend who was not able to join us at the reunion and lost her life to cancer soon after it:

A lady who lived on our way to school didn't like anyone near her property. One day we stopped nearby to play with an old wooden wheelchair we found. She chased us away with her broom. The next day, Sister Marciana came and got me out of mass to tell me we were reported for being disrespectful. I told her it wasn't me, it must have been my sister, she just got us confused.

There was an advantage to being part of those big families!

Danger Grows

Despite feeling safe during the May Procession, the streets were starting to get dangerous. One of Laura's older brothers played the organ at our church while he was in high school. Her family lived very close to the church, only a couple of blocks away. One night, as her brother was walking home late, he was attacked. Six black boys he didn't know jumped out of some bushes. It was dark and it happened so fast he couldn't identify them. Laura's parents were pretty shaken up and called the police. He wasn't hurt badly enough to be taken to the hospital, but he was beaten up. After that happened, Laura remembers hearing her parents talking about moving away. They didn't want to, but now felt they had no choice. They decided to wait two years until Laura finished eighth grade, which was a big deal in our school. Laura was very grateful for that but admits that she and her family were more afraid during those last years; she wasn't allowed to walk alone in the neighborhood. There started to be talk about gangs of black kids forming, that maybe it was a gang that beat up her brother, but no one was ever caught.

Eileen had trouble with one of our classmates that same year, sixth grade:

> "I remember Paula Wilson waiting for me after school to beat me up. She just started waiting for me every day, right outside the building. I didn't tell anyone for a long time, because she said: 'Don't tell or I'll beat you worse.' She'd pull my hair and take my books and throw them on the ground, that sort of thing. So, I started leaving a different way or waiting around inside until she left. When I did tell my mom, she went up to the school to report it and she was very dissatisfied with the answer. The principal, Sister Thea, said, 'Now we all have to get along, Mrs. Miller.' And my Mom said, 'Well, that's fine with me, but my daughter is getting beaten up every

day.' They just said we all need to get along—like I started it or something. That's when my mom stopped volunteering; before that my mom had been in the school all the time: she volunteered at the library, she worked in the office, they even asked her to teach. But from that day on she said, 'I'm done.' She was so mad. I don't know why Paula picked me. She always really struggled in school, I do remember that. And I never did. So, I don't know if that was part of the problem. She was always pulling my hair. I had that long straight hair; maybe she didn't like that. I was a tiny little kid; Paula was a big girl."

Sheila was also afraid often in those middle years, but not of the kids in our school. She and her siblings walked home for lunch and they lived far from school, so they would be walking back while the public grammar school, Avalon Park, was letting out for lunch:

"There were many times where I was minding my own business and I would get harassed by black girls, saying, 'What you looking at girl?'—pushing me over, off the sidewalk. I would try all I could not to have eye contact or anything, but it would happen. And it was very worrisome when I would have my little brother with me. I had to protect him. This was starting in sixth grade, so he was just eight years old. By the time we got home and ate our lunch and headed back it was late. I never got back in time to play on the playground. At this point my mom was still thinking everything was fine."

Beth lived close to Caldwell, the public grammar school on the opposite end of the neighborhood:

"I remember having to run home because I didn't want to run into those public-school girls. They were dismissed 10 or 15 minutes after us and, if I waited too long, you know we all liked to stand around and talk and hang out before heading home, and if I waited too long, I'd run into them and probably get my hair pulled or get knocked over. It just wasn't really safe."

Apparently, the public schools intentionally let their students out at different times from us to reduce the chances that they would run into the kids from our school. It might have just been an attempt at keeping down the sheer numbers of kids on the loose, but I wonder if it only made us all leerier of each other. I lived only a block from Avalon Park School. I don't remember ever running into public-school kids at lunchtime but sometimes saw them after school.

My sisters and I took weekly piano lessons from Mrs. Rose, who lived about two blocks from our house. When I started my lessons, in second grade, Terry and I went together, one of us waiting impatiently while the other had her lesson. Once I got into fourth or fifth grade, I was allowed to walk to and from my lesson alone. One time when I was walking alone, I ran into some kids on their way home from the public school. It was late afternoon, in the winter, starting to get dark. A little boy, who was black, walked directly towards me and reached his hand up to touch my coat – right at the level of my stomach, or maybe a bit lower. He seemed younger than me, but he may have just been short. He said something I couldn't quite hear, then laughed and ran off. I was taken aback and a little frightened but just kept walking and never told anyone. I don't know that he targeted me because I was white or just because I was a girl—and probably looked afraid. I wonder now if he was imitating the way older black kids taunted us.

Sheila had a problem with a little boy at church one day. There were some younger kids sitting behind her, black kids, that were taunting her through the whole mass. She was afraid and didn't think they were just mouthing off. When she left the church after mass one of the boys jumped on her back. She was by herself and remembers adults walking by looking at them like they were just playing. She was afraid. This kid would not leave her alone, but she didn't think to cry out or ask the adults for help. He was the younger brother of someone she knew, not in our class, but in our school. He wanted to beat her up because of something that had happened between Sheila and his older sister. She doesn't have a clear memory of how this incident ended, but can still picture the adults, black and white, walking right by as she was in distress. Today I would say the adults might have been hesitant to interfere for fear of being attacked themselves. I don't know why they didn't help Sheila back in 1966. Maybe they didn't want to admit that little black kids and little white kids didn't always get along. I wonder if they would have intervened if the kid who jumped on her had been white.

These episodes all ended without serious consequences, but there were dangerous things happening nearby. When I was about twelve, a girl disappeared in a park a few miles from our house. I guess I heard about it from my friends. After dinner one evening, I was sitting at the table with my mother and oldest sister who was an "adult," as far as I was concerned. If I was 12, she was 19 then, so she was sort of an adult. We always, always, always had dinner as a family at five o'clock. My dad would sometimes work after dinner, at his desk in the basement, but he was at the table for dinner and we were not to be late. I guess he had gone to his desk when this scene happened. I'm not sure where my other sister was, but I vividly remember my older sister and my mom talking about how sad it was that this girl had been hurt. I asked them how she was hurt, and they told me she was molested. I told them that my friends said that meant the man did something to her body. My mother asked me if I remembered what I'd read in the book she gave me about how babies were made. She said that was what the man had done to this little girl. I actually think the girl was murdered, also, but this is the part I remember. It was very scary for me to think something like that had happened to a girl about my age and not very far from where I lived. I don't think this incident had anything

51

to do with the changes going on in the neighborhood. Both the victim and the perpetrator were white, as far as I know. But this happened during the time that danger seemed to be growing overall and increased our level of fear. I remember being haunted by this for awhile, although I don't remember it changing my behavior. It did give me one more reason to be cautious in our park, while I was still allowed to go there.

I will never forget one morning during the summer after sixth grade. When I got up, I found my mother in the vinyl booth we called the "breakfast nook" in our recently renovated kitchen. It was now a tasteful, very 1960s, pink. Mom was having her morning nourishment—coffee and a cigarette—and had the newspaper open on the table. My mother was an avid newspaper reader her entire life. There were photos of eight women on the front page. I don't recall what she told me then, but I know that there was an eerie feeling around the house and the neighborhood for several days. Eight student nurses had been murdered in a townhouse three miles from our school. The murderer, mass murderer we would learn to call him, was caught four days later, after being taken to the emergency room bleeding from a suicide attempt. A ninth nurse had been able to hide all night under a bed and give an eye witness description. I'm sure we were all relieved he had been caught. Evil, for us at that moment, was a white man named Richard Speck.

Chapter 3

SEVENTH GRADE

Despite the fearful summer of 1966, we entered seventh grade with a sense of excitement—we were now the understudies for the preeminent eighth graders. A few select seventh-grade girls got to be cheerleaders. Girls could also join the choral, even those of us who could not carry a tune. Seventh-grade boys could try out for the sports teams; sports were a very important part of our lives.

The New Church Rules

Our seventh-grade year was when I first remember the nuns, at least some of them, starting to wear more modern habits with skirts that showed part of their legs and shorter veils with some hair showing. We had always wondered if they even had hair. We girls didn't have to cover our heads in church any more, either. Not that we ever really did. We wore "chapel veils" which were lace doilies about six inches wide that we bobby-pinned on top of our heads. Sometimes we even folded them in half or quarters, to keep them from messing up our carefully coifed hair. If you lost, or more likely forgot, your chapel veil, you could get away with pinning a Kleenex on your head. Not really in the spirit of piety, but it met the letter of the law. Now even that meager effort was not required.

These were some of the most visible, to us, impacts of the Second Vatican Council, known as "Vatican II." The biggest change had happened a couple of years earlier, when the priests started facing us during mass and speaking to us in English. This was pretty radical stuff, but it was the sixties; the world was changing all around us, why not inside our church?

One of our teachers that year was memorable, too. Her name was Sister Blanche, but she had been given the nickname "Sarge" by students before us, and we saw no reason to change it. She was loud and even bossier than most nuns. She claimed not to know our names; instead, she called all the boys Oscar and the girls Oswella.

This was also about the time some of the nuns at our school got into the "Up with People" craze, probably after the 1966 television special that was broadcast to 100 million people.[4] They would assemble us all in the school basement so we could learn the songs we had heard on television. Here is the main anthem of the movement, off the top of my head, fifty years later: "Up, up with people. There's people wherever you go. Up, up with people, the best kind of folks that we know. If more people were for people, for people everywhere, there'd be a lot less people to worry about and a lot more people who care." What does that even mean? Despite its message of peace and unity, Richard Williams, one of our African-American classmates, has the following memory of one of the songs we were taught by the nuns:

> "We were singing 'What Color is God's Skin' and when we got to the words 'It's black, brown, yellow . . .' some white kids would shout 'white' when we got to the word white and then some black kids shouted 'black' when we got to that word. Pretty discomfiting scene inside a Catholic school."

Our more formal choral choices were embracing broader themes, also. I remember going to the big convention center downtown for a city-wide choral event and singing a song called "Shalom." Hebrew had not been part of our curriculum before.

About this time, our beloved Father Kelley died and was replaced with Father Kozak, who was not Irish, which was radical for our parish. He was white, but he sometimes wore a dashiki, a colorful African robe, instead of his black cassock. We didn't know what it was and did not relate it to the growing African-American population in the parish. We just thought he was weird. He was quite young compared to our other priests, having just come out of seminary, probably under thirty. The other priests always seemed much older. Father Kelley was actually only in his forties when he died, but that was ancient to us.

As Monsignor Walsh had feared, church attendance did drop off; some of our new neighbors were not Catholic. The African-American families that joined the parish also had fewer children than most of the white families, so class sizes started to decline. (The average family, when the parish was predominantly Irish, had about six kids.) The smaller class sizes were no doubt a relief to the nuns who, at the school's peak, were teaching forty to fifty kids in each room. We never had teacher's assistants; those nuns, and a few lay teachers, still had a strong control over us, even the preteen boys.

By seventh grade, we girls had also transitioned out of those navy-blue jumpers and into blue-plaid-pleated-wool skirts, worn with white blouses, knee-high socks and loafers. We called them penny loafers because they had a slot where you could insert a penny, which we usually did. As mini-skirts became the norm outside of school, we would "roll up" those uniform skirts at their waistbands whenever we were out of sight of the nuns (and our parents). This made them much shorter than we were allowed to wear them. I'm sure it looked bulky and, well, ridiculous, but we thought it showed how cool we were—and rebellious.

The Groundsmen (Not a Gang)

The teenage boys in the parish formed a loosely-organized group they called the Groundsmen. It sounded like a gang to me, but they consider it a "social and athletic club." The "grounds" referred to our playground, the place where we used to scrape our knees falling off the merry-go-round and "freeze" when the bell rang. We were fortunate to have a full-sized gym in that repurposed church building that held our kindergarten classroom, which was right across the street from the playground. The boys hung out on the playground while waiting for the gym to open and met there when they wanted to go somewhere, like the beach, together. No one seems to remember when they started calling it the "grounds," or who came up with the term, but it certainly sounded cooler than "the playground," especially to teenage boys who wanted to sound grown up, and maybe just a little bit tough.

The Groundsmen was started by the Felicitas eighth-grade classes of the early sixties, a few years before ours, but others joined later, younger kids and kids from other parishes who went to high school with Felicitas kids. The Groundsmen were all white and you had to be accepted by the group; not just anybody could be a Groundsman. To me, the name "Groundsmen" just sounded like a gang name and there was certainly trouble associated with them from time to time. The black kids from the public schools in the neighborhood and from other neighborhoods nearby knew that this group of white teenage boys hung out on the "grounds," so they were an easy-to-find target. Any time any of the Groundsmen got into an altercation or felt they were under attack, they would run to the O'Brien's basement because there were always more boys hanging out there, and they were more than ready to go out to defend their fellow Groundsmen.

A Groundsman a few years older than me told me a story about one such event that could have escalated into something tragic. Word had gotten out that the boys from Avalon Park, the nearby public school, who were mostly, if not all, black, wanted to "take over" the St. Felicitas gym. Apparently, the public school didn't have its own gym. I'm not sure why they couldn't just use the gym at the park, but the story goes that the Groundsmen were going to defend their territory, and that included the gym at our school. They put out a call for backup to their high school friends, so lots of boys were there that night, 40 or 50, hiding behind the school and the gym—there were several dark corners and hiding places between the buildings. It was about seven o'clock in the evening, but it was summer, so still light out.

The plan was to bait the public-school kids by putting a couple of the Groundsmen out front, visible, acting as if they didn't know about the planned "takeover." Then, when the black kids arrived, the rest of the white kids would come out of hiding and fight them off. Or something like that. I'm not sure how coherent the plan was and, luckily, it never got put into action. A large group of black teens, more than 50, a really big group, and probably all boys, did show up. As they were crossing busy 83rd Street, still a block away from the grounds, but visible to the boys who were the decoys out front, the police arrived—lots of them. More cops than kids. All the kids took off—both the public-school kids and the Groundsmen and their friends—knowing they were all in big trouble if they got caught.

Two of the Groundsmen that were there, brothers, were the sons of a Chicago cop. Their dad wasn't there that night but certainly heard about it. He told them the next morning that they had been very lucky the police showed up. The Groundsmen had been badly outnumbered and some of the public-school kids had some sort of homemade weapons called zip guns. The boys don't remember being punished and don't think that anyone, even the "gun" wielders, got into any real trouble. They also don't know how the police found out, but I'm sure a lot of St. Felicitas parents were relieved that they did. Following this incident, Monsignor Walsh floated the idea of a basketball league to be hosted at the St. Felicitas gym that would include the public-school kids—an olive branch that he perhaps hoped would mend any rivalry between the two groups of teens who shared the neighborhood. A few meetings were held, but the league never materialized.

High school boys from our parish joined sports leagues and played all over the city. Their teams were always called the Groundsmen. One of the older Groundsmen made some home movies under the Groundsmen name. The films were creative projects and included African-American kids from our parish in their "casts." Anyone who was hanging out at the grounds the day the movie was made might land a part in the production. There was even one girl, someone's girlfriend, who was invited to appear, cast as the girlfriend, of course. I learned about these movies as an adult, when I happened to be in town for the fiftieth-birthday party of one of the Groundsmen, a classmate of mine. The movies were on in the background of his party and people were watching, laughing, and remembering the fun they had in "the good old days." And yes, they still consider themselves Groundsmen today.

What's a Girl to Do

While the boys were hanging out at the grounds, we girls hung out a block away at our neighborhood corner store, The Little Del, and a commercial building across the street from the store that we called "the instrument building." It wasn't a retail business, so it was quiet there. It had a sign saying it was some sort of business with the word instrument in it. I never cared what type of instruments it meant; we just knew that it had a nice stoop that we could sit on and no one ever came out of the building to ask why we were there. A group of teenagers, with no reason to do business with them, sitting there for what seems now like hours at a time, in the afternoon after school. And they never bothered us. Nor did the police, although I'm sure many passed by the instrument building; it was on a major street in an urban neighborhood which was starting to be dangerous. In those days, kids could hang out in public places without attracting any sort of attention or concern.

The Little Del was the smallest store I've ever seen, something akin to a New York City bodega, possibly even smaller. In my memory, it was about 10 feet wide with dry goods on shelves completely covering one wall and a counter along the other wall. There was barely room for two people to pass in the single aisle. Since it was a "deli," there was probably fresh food or cold cuts in the counter displays, but we went in for just three things – ice-cold pop in six-ounce bottles, potato chips in single-serving bags and "penny" candy, which was kept behind the counter. The clerks were infinitely patient, (much like those at our bakery), taking orders from children who wanted two cents worth of flying saucers and a jawbreaker.

There were plenty of places around the school building and on the playground where we could have hung out. I'm not sure why we chose the Del and the instrument building instead, but I can

58

guess we wanted to be out of range of the nuns and priests who also lived on the church/school complex, and away from the boys. We liked boys but didn't really know how to talk to them. We weren't doing anything bad; we were just teenagers who wanted to gossip and waste time and didn't want anyone to know what we were up to. The only trouble we caused was when we wanted to cross between our two hangouts. They were separated by Stony Island, a six-lane boulevard. Of course, we did not walk to the corner where there was a light; we ran across in the middle of the block, dodging traffic. We were thirteen years old and therefore invincible. Luckily, no one was ever hurt, but I do wonder why motorists never complained.

School Demographics

Quite a few more black classmates joined us in the seventh grade; they now made up 20 percent of the class. We all remember Richard Williams because he was a football and basketball star. Or maybe we remember him because he was so good looking. Since he was part of the football team, he just seemed like one of the guys, but he was not invited to join the Groundsmen. He does appear in one of their movies, though. Martha Edwards, on the other hand, was not as easily accepted. Laura remembers being afraid of her, probably because Martha was so much bigger than most of us. I wonder now if she might have been older and just behind academically. Laura was always short, she was only five foot two as an adult, and Martha was kind of a tough girl, what we would now call a bully. One day in school, Martha dropped a tissue on the floor and taunted Laura, saying "Laura, pick up my Kleenex!" It was mild aggression, but bullying nonetheless, and all these years later, Laura still remembers being afraid of Martha. On a lighter note, Beth remembers Martha because they both brought their lunch to school on occasion and Martha would eat sardines out of a can. This was something very unusual to Beth, who was raised on PB&J just like I was.

In seventh grade, as we entered our teens, we girls were in

our own world, just trying to have fun with our friends—dancing in my basement at pajama parties, celebrating each other's birthdays, putting each other's hair in rollers. We were so involved in our own dramas that we didn't really notice how much things were changing around us. Or maybe we intentionally blocked it out. Our group of close friends was segregated, the black girls we had befriended in fourth, fifth, and sixth grades were not a part of the clique we formed in seventh grade, the group that is still friends today.

A few of us remember neighbors who moved out in the middle of the night around this time. One day a white family lived next door, the next day there was an African-American family living there. We didn't mind that the new neighbors were black; we just didn't know how it happened so quickly. We usually didn't even know the houses were for sale. One morning you woke up and you had new neighbors and the old neighbors were gone. Beth shared a story about this phenomenon:

> "There was a family that lived behind us, they had a daughter my age who went to public school, and I played with her. They were very active in the Civil Rights Movement; they would go downtown and demonstrate, and they always said, 'You have to welcome people of all colors, all races. Don't panic, it'll be okay.' And, wouldn't you know, they were about the first to move. And it really irked my mother, because that woman was always on our block preaching that nobody should be moving. And it was one of those overnight things—the van pulled up at night, they loaded their stuff and they were gone. They didn't want anyone to know that they were selling to African Americans. They didn't want to get the flack. I remember my Mom being so mad. Their daughter was my friend, but I never heard from her again."

Mother Nature

The planet was also acting strangely during our seventh-grade year. In January we had what was then the biggest snow storm in the history of the city. Actually, it still holds the record for the most snow from one storm—23 inches fell in just over 24 hours. It had been 65 degrees two days earlier. That suddenness made it difficult to cope with. School was cancelled for a few days – that had never happened before. We were used to walking to school through snow and ice in freezing temperatures. That's what tights were for. When we were younger, we even wore wool pants under our uniform skirts and took them off when we got to school. Our classrooms each had small rooms on the side, called cloakrooms, that served as closets for all of our coats, boots, hats, scarves, etc. Those rooms always smelled of wet wool.

The storm of 1967 was a challenge, even for the well-organized snow removal crews in Chicago. I remember my dad walking in that snow for two miles to open his grocery store. He couldn't possibly get his car out of the garage at our house and the side streets had not been plowed yet. People were making an attempt to shovel their sidewalks, so I guess he got through the three long blocks from our house to 79th Street using those cleared sidewalks and climbing over drifts. He then trudged down the middle of normally busy 79th Street; there was only a small area cleared. I guess there were really no cars on the road that day, just my dad and the snow plows. In parts of Chicago that weekend, stores were being looted, possibly out of the general unruliness of mobs, but also because the stores were closed, and people needed food. That's why my dad wanted to open his store. The storm came without warning, so no one had stocked up. Beth remembers walking with her sister through snow banks higher than they were tall to the grocery store closest to her house and finding the shelves empty of fresh food. She and her siblings had to drink powdered milk for a few days. They did not enjoy the experience.

I have pictures of our family's two dogs, miniature poodles, standing on drifts after the storm and looking over our backyard fence, which was normally way over their heads. I'm sure I went out and jumped in a drift or two, but I have always been a weather wimp, so I'm pretty sure I spent most of the time in the house on the phone with my friends. As teenagers, we were not as excited about missing school as the little kids were. It interrupted our all-important social lives. Other important things were also interrupted—commerce, transportation. Buses and cars were stranded in banks of snow. Twenty-six people died as a result of that storm.

Less than three months later, Mother Nature battered Chicago again, this time with a tornado. It was a Friday afternoon and Beth and I were at our sewing lessons at the park. When we headed home for dinner, the sky was a weird green color, and it was raining. I lived close to the park, so made it home before the storm really kicked in. Beth lived farther and ended up spending some time hanging on to a light pole in an alley on the way to her house, so that she wouldn't get blown away. She remembers electrical wires flying around overhead and her mom, at her back door, waiting, absolutely terrified. Beth was the only one of her ten children not home during the worst part of the storm. I remember seeing Beth at mass the next morning. She had pieces of hail still in the pockets of her coat. I guess they left it outside overnight because it was so wet.

My family was sitting around the dinner table when the storm hit. It was five o'clock and nothing delayed supper time at our house. Our dining room had a whole wall of windows; we could see the storm picking up. At some point, probably when he heard that roaring train noise tornados make, my dad decided we should head to the basement. Good old Chicago bungalows had big basements. Ours had a few windows but they were made of glass block, so we were pretty safe down there. We couldn't really see the storm any more though, so my dad went out the basement door and up the stairs into the yard to take a look. I can still picture him standing there, framed in the doorway, the storm going on behind him. It was dark outside—and loud—a real "Wizard of Oz" moment. I do not think my mother was very happy with him for risking his life like that.

No one near us was hurt, but a suburb less than ten miles away got hit hard. Thirty-three people died there. The roof collapsed on a skating rink full of teenagers, which is what I remember most, being a teenager myself at the time. There were also school buses and cars tossed around and many buildings were destroyed. A few trees in our neighborhood went down and some roofs were damaged, but, as tornadoes go, we got off easy. Modern meteorology is much better at predicting tornados, but this one hit without warning. Chicago is in the Midwest and not immune to storms, but it's not as common as, say, Oklahoma, where I've had the luck to live through three more tornados over the years since then. In 1967, "The Wizard of Oz" was the only knowledge I had of tornados. We watched it every year, mostly because part of it was in "living color."

Picking Cheerleaders

Despite these weather challenges, spring to us meant the end of basketball season, and time to pick cheerleaders for the next football season. Sports were a big deal in our parish, football especially. For the girls that meant cheering on the boys who played. We were certainly fine with that; it was our honor and duty—and might lead to romance, who knows? We didn't have fancy uniforms; we wore what we could afford: red wool skirts (often hand-me-downs from our sisters) with basic white sweatshirts adorned with the letter "F" made out of felt we cut ourselves. We had some great cheers, though. "Two bits, four bits, six bits, a dollar, all for Felicitas stand up and holler!" was a biggie. Pretty original, right? We were not acrobatic, or anything like that. We just stood on the sidelines and yelled a lot. And it was heaven.

Like most things, football would be best in eighth grade, when our boys would be the oldest and therefore the stars. But we got a preview in the seventh grade. I'm not sure how the seventh-grade boys got to play on the team, but there was a tradition of allowing only ten seventh-grade girls onto the cheerleading squad.

They were "picked" by girls going into the eighth grade—the girls who had been "picked" the year before. Each soon-to-be eighth-grade girl could pick one soon-to-be seventh-grade girl and, given the big families in the parish, the picking rights were quite often specific to families. If a Cullnan had picked you and there was another Cullnan coming up behind you, you picked her. Seems fair, right? As a seventh grader, being picked was something very important. It made a major difference in your life. You were somebody. If you didn't get picked? I can't even think about it.

Going into seventh grade I was twelve, so this all seemed very important, almost magical to me, one of those life passages that can change the course of your future. I had a sister two years older, so there was a girl picked by her willing to pick me. What luck! I never felt like a part of the "in-crowd" before, but my sister was, so I managed to slip in. My parents must have planned my birth to coincide with this key life passage. I didn't think about the black girls in our class whose sisters weren't in our school in time to get into the great picking order. Not that their sisters would have gotten picked if they had been there in time. Nothing against them, we just had a system and it had been in place since the dawn of time, for all we knew. We certainly saw no reason to change it now that we were finally the ones coming up—the "pickees"—and we certainly didn't want to share, let alone lose, our chance. Somehow, the system was allowed to play out the year we were picked, perhaps because it was 1966 and there were not very many black girls in our class yet.

In the spring of seventh grade we progressed to being the "pickers," a position of power, finally. The selection process took place just before school let out for the summer, so that the pickees could revel in their good fortune over the summer and make whatever arrangements were necessary to ensure they had uniforms and were able to attend practice and football games come fall. Each of us made a selection, but it was a group process, no use having any duplicates on the list. Collusion was encouraged.

For some unmemorable reason, I was given the honor of taking the list of fortunate sixth grader "pickees" into the sixth-grade classrooms. I thought I was a real big deal. Remember the scene in the movie "A Christmas Story," when Ralphie imagines how his teacher will praise his composition, giving it an A +++++? That is the feeling I had entering the classroom and approaching Sister Mary Jean to tell her the purpose of my visit. Like Ralphie's, my experience didn't go as planned. Not even close. Sister Mary Jean did not greet me with open arms and sing my praises for being the bringer of good tidings to a few lucky girls in her class. She gave me a look that sent shivers through me, as only a nun's look can. She said something to the effect of "this won't do," and sent me back to my classroom. My friends were all there—awaiting my triumphant return with the thanks of the minions we had chosen. All I could tell them was that Sister Mary Jean had the list and did not seem happy about it. I was crestfallen, a failure at such an honorable task.

A few days later we would hear the fate of our list—and our fair and noble process. It was over—for good. We seventh graders would not have our chance to benevolently select our successors. Instead, the sisters had decreed that any sixth grader who wanted to be a cheerleader in seventh grade was welcome to join, just like all eighth graders could join.

It took a while before we realized why this had happened. Under our system we assumed that the girls who were not chosen knew they were not part of the in-crowd and didn't expect to be, right? Our white classmates knew this was the way the world worked at St. Felicitas. It must be the new girls who brought this apocalypse upon us. Or maybe it was just our teachers' sense of what was right and truly fair. I get it now, but at thirteen, I had not developed much of a social conscience, at least not enough to see injustice in a system as sacred as cheerleader picking. We, last year's chosen ones, were not happy with this usurping of our authority, and we were starting to realize that our world was changing. Perhaps eighth grade would not be ours to rule. In case you are wondering, when football season began the next fall, although all twenty-one of the white girls in our eighth-grade class were cheerleaders, only four of our fourteen black female classmates chose to join us. I don't have the statistics for the seventh-grade class, but we certainly had a very large cheerleading squad that year—more like a crowd than a squad, I'd say. We probably outnumbered the football players.

Neighborhood Danger

Sheila's house was deep into Marynook, far from the busier streets and our school, near one of the park entrances. She remembers walking home after school one time and passing the opening to the walkway into the park. Suddenly, a group of about a dozen black girls, around her age, came out of the walkway. She was alone and was immediately anxious. She didn't know them, and they were moving fast. They were on the opposite side of the street, so she thought she could just keep walking by, but they crossed over and, as she passed them, one of them tried to trip her. She didn't fall down; she turned around and said, instinctively, "Now why did you do that?" This questioning led the girl to slap Sheila in the face. Sheila had heard stories of kids getting beaten up by this time, a friend of her sister's had gotten "jumped" right near this same entrance, so, although she felt humiliated after being tripped and slapped for no reason, she just walked away. They continued to taunt her but did not attack her again. She and her sister experienced other, similar occurrences, times when they were followed, taunted and afraid, often when walking from school to their home, tucked away as it was along the winding streets of Marynook. They told their parents, who initially questioned what their daughters did to provoke such attacks. Her parents were trying to ensure that their children did not develop racial prejudice. As Sheila tells it:

> "The rule in our house was we were never to use the 'n' word. My parent's message was, 'They're people. Accept them.' That's the message I got."

Sheila told this story of another incident that year, this time with a girl who went to our school, but was older than us:

> "Donna Gates followed my sister Julie, who was in the eighth grade, home from school, taunting her. After she got home, Julie and I went up to the dime store on 87th Street. Donna followed us, still taunting, wanting to fight. We ran into our older sister, Mary, at the store. Right at that moment, Donna punched Julie in the back, because Julie wouldn't turn around and fight her. Mary had a bag with cans in it that she just bought at the grocery store, and she swung around with the cans. This is one thing I always admired my sister Mary for. I don't know if she connected or not, but Donna was on top of her in a second, like a wild cat. Fortunately, the manager of the dime store, who happened to be black, came out and stopped it. My mom was very upset about this, especially since Donna's family lived near us and she went to our school. So, my mom went to see Donna's mother and said, 'Your daughter did this,' but the mom said, 'My daughter didn't do that.' Donna had lied to her mom and said she was home watching her little brother. I think my parents were very open-minded, and maybe they stayed open-minded, but they finally realized their kids weren't causing the trouble; it was not something we were doing.
>
> "One of the problems was that I didn't know how to cope with someone wanting to fight with me. Girls didn't fight. There was no need to know how to fight. I hadn't encountered it before and did not know how to react."

The event that really got Sheila's father's attention was when her oldest sister, Mary, was attacked in the park by a black boy who lived right next door to them. He and another boy knocked her down and jumped on her. Mary looked right at him and said she knew him, called him by name, which surprised him. Sheila thinks that is why the boys let Mary go. They were about her age, early high school at the time. She went right home and told her parents. Her older brother ran out of the house and tried to find them, but he never did. Her parents spoke to the parents of the boy, their next-door neighbors, but didn't report the incident to the police. After the attack, her parents started to see that the chasing and hitting was not just child's play, it could turn much worse. This time, the boys involved didn't go to our school, but they lived in our neighborhood, in this case, right next door. It was now too much to ignore.

Denial by trusted adults was common during the early years of the racial transition in our neighborhood. When kids would tell their parents of being followed, chased, even hit, the first reaction was often, "What did you do to provoke it?" I don't recall ever telling my parents any of the stories I heard or things that had happened to me, but my friends got this reaction often, from parents, teachers and other adults they told in their attempts to thwart actions by other kids that they knew were wrong.

The boys in our parish knew a little more about how to fight, or at least thought they did. One day an older boy from our school got jumped by two black kids in the neighborhood. One of those kids was Jeff, who the Groundsmen knew because he lived right near some of our classmates, although he didn't go to our school. When the white boy, Robert, ran to the school gym, he found several of his friends there playing basketball. One of them told me what happened next, as a group of white kids from our school took off to find Jeff and his friend. They found them standing on the stairs in front of one of the neighborhood's many old brick bungalows. Jeff was now holding a baseball bat; his friend had a small wooden club. One of the Felicitas boys, Alan, walked right up the stairs and asked them why they hit Robert. Alan started punching Jeff while the other boys started hitting Jeff's friend. A window shattered on the porch, startling everyone. The Felicitas boys ran back to the gym. Nobody was seriously injured, but Alan and the other Groundsmen were determined not to let Jeff and his friends get the upper hand in their neighborhood.

Back at the gym, after the danger had passed, the boys felt obligated to go back to the house with the broken window and tell the owners that they would pay for the damage. Maybe it was obligation, or maybe just fear that the nuns would find out. The nuns always found out. At this time, the boys still feared the wrath of the nuns at least as much as that of the black kids who threatened them in the streets. As they were knocking on the door of the house with the broken window, they heard a commotion coming from down the block. Soon they saw a large group of black youths, at least twenty, coming towards them. Terribly outnumbered and now truly fearful, they quickly ran back to the gym and barricaded themselves inside. After a few minutes, another Felicitas boy started pounding on the gym door and was let in. He told them he only got away from the black youths when the one closest to him slipped and fell, a common occurrence during these street scuffles. Rocks started bouncing off the open windows of the gym, with a few falling to the floor around the boys, who remained huddled inside until the group of black youths gave up and left them alone.

About a week later, while walking from his house to the playground, Alan ran into Jeff and his friend. Jeff taunted Alan, asking if he remembered him. Alan was not afraid until he saw another black youth on a bike about to cut off his only route of escape. Alan pulled out one of the "weapons" he now carried daily, a dog's choke chain, and starting swinging it towards Jeff, who backed off. Alan also carried an open pocket knife. He no longer felt safe between his home and our school, three blocks away.

A different kind of attack was being experienced by the girls. Laura remembers a day she and a few of our friends were walking home from Sears. Sears was another favorite hangout of ours. It was on 79th street, so pretty close to my house, but several blocks from our school, on the very edge of the territory we were allowed to travel, so not visited quite as often as our other hangouts. This day was in the summer after seventh grade, 1967, so the girls all had short shorts on, being in tune with the fashions of the day.

Two older black boys were walking toward them. By this time, we had all started having a sense of apprehension any time we saw a group of African-American kids coming toward us, wondering, "What are they going to do? What is going to happen this time?" As the two boys passed the girls, one of them reached out and grabbed Laura and Eileen "down on our private parts," as Laura described it. Just reached out, took two hands and touched both of them. Laura recalls:

> "I was stunned. He was older than us, he was a big tall kid, I'd say he was a teenager, 17 or 18; he was big. We didn't know what to say, I don't think we said anything. I don't know if I told my mom about this one. I was probably too embarrassed. You got to the point where you kind of hid things because our parents would just put more restrictions on us. So, I did keep some things to myself."

But it was still summer, and we were still determined to have fun. Our favorite radio station, WLS, declared it "Super Summer." I have a button from the station that shows a sun wearing sunglasses emblazoned with that slogan. I also have one of the all-important "Top Forty" lists that I regularly walked to Sears to pick up. It came out every week and was as important to me as the daily headlines were to my mother. The one I kept is special because it is signed by the WLS disc jockeys. My friends and I made a trip downtown to visit the studio that weekend. On June 30, 1967 the top song was "Windy" by the Association.

At number seven that week was "If you're going to San Francisco, be sure to wear some flowers in your hair." Over a hundred thousand young people, many not much older than us, did just that, descending on Haight-Ashbury for "The Summer of Love," introducing us Catholic school girls to hippie culture, at least what could be seen on the television news. That same summer also brought the bloodiest race riots in history to Detroit, along with riots in over 150 other U.S. cities, adding the label "long, hot, summer" to the "summer of love." From my view of all this, on television, America looked schizophrenic – hippies celebrating peace and love in a beautiful park followed by National Guardsmen chasing blacks with burning buildings in the background, then there were the daily body counts from Vietnam. The war had now reached its peak, 500,000 American troops were there in 1967.

One of the war casualties that year was a St. Felicitas kid, a boy my sister Connie knew. Lance Corporal John Joseph Bryar, a United States Marine, was killed in action in South Vietnam on March 23, 1967. He was 22 years old. A young man who worked for my father was drafted around this time and he also died in Vietnam, about a year later. When I looked him up in the National Archives database, I discovered that he was born the same day as my sister. They were both 20 at the time that he died. That is the only day I can remember seeing my big sister cry.

National news was made in our neighborhood that summer, too, when Muhammed Ali married his second wife in a brick bungalow a few blocks from Beth's house. I don't remember how long he lived in the neighborhood, but my friends recall sightings of him. Such sightings were not only remarkable because of his fame in the ring, but because his wife and other women who were seen with them wore traditional Muslim dress, something we had never seen. They looked almost like our nuns, except that none of our nuns were black.

Even closer to home, we lost a classmate that summer. He was swimming at a beach on Lake Michigan with his friends, a short distance from the area patrolled by lifeguards. For some reason, he decided to swim out beyond where red and white buoys bobbed to mark it safe for swimming. His friends said that he had on his black leather combat boots. They could tell he was in trouble and tried to swim out to him, but they couldn't reach him. A police boat came by and pulled him out, but it was too late. I heard about it when Beth called me early the next morning. Her brother was one of the boys at the scene. I'm ashamed to say I burst out laughing at the news. The boy who died was something of a troublemaker and I found the idea of him drowning absurd; it must be a joke. It was true, though, and most of our class was in the pews of St. Felicitas for his funeral a few days later. Beth recalls some boys we didn't know, who she believes were members of one of Chicago's street gangs, sitting together at the back of the church. Our deceased classmate was rumored to be a part of a gang. A real one.

This tragic event happened just a week or so before the beginning of eighth grade, the year we had been anticipating since we entered Kindergarten together all those many years before.

Chapter 4

EIGHTH GRADE

Finally—Eighth Grade! At St. Felicitas, eighth grade was a really big deal. We had been looking forward to it forever and expected it to be wonderful, glorious, life changing—because we would be the stars of the show. Eighth grade to us was the equivalent of being a senior in high school for other kids. We had been in the same school, with many of the same classmates, following and being followed by siblings, through years of tradition: kindergarten with its special aproned uniforms and play areas, second grade, that First Communion year of study and holiness, up through Girl Scouts, Confirmation, turkey raffles and many, many masses—all leading up to the penultimate eighth-grade year. Seventh grade gave us a bit of a preview; a few boys made the cut for the sports teams and some lucky girls were picked to be cheerleaders, but we were still the understudies, watching the eighth graders have their glory year and waiting patiently (somewhat) for ours.

Our class had shrunk from a high of 107 in grade three to 76, so we only needed two classrooms. One of our nuns was very young and claims she was afraid of us. The feeling was mutual—and she was the one with the big stick, literally. She told Eileen years later that she sometimes had to soak her hands in cold water at lunch—after beating the boys who had misbehaved. The other nun was older and, well, larger. My sister still holds a grudge for the way she was treated by this nun, but I remember her as being okay. Although I wasn't really afraid of her, she did keep me after class one of the first days of school, for talking in class. I had never been in trouble before, so was quite surprised to be singled out this way. I think she remembered my sister and wanted to be sure I wasn't like her. My sister was not as meek as I was.

Football & Music

In the fall of eighth grade "our" boys were the stars of the football team and "we" girls were in charge of cheerleading and arranging the parties that were held after every game. The parties were more important to the girls than the games. We were ready for romance. Although these parties took place in our family homes, they were generally in basements with very little, if any, adult supervision. We girls danced to the "fast" songs of the 60s together, but, eventually, a slow song would come on. "Cherish" by The Association was our favorite that year. Often, about the time the music slowed down, the lights would go down, making the atmosphere much more conducive for brave thirteen-year-old boys to ask nervous thirteen-year-old girls to dance. I'm sure there were hormones involved, but I just remember being scared I would do or say the wrong thing—or that I would not be asked to dance. Being a wallflower was the ultimate embarrassment, even if the room was dark. There was touching involved, hand on shoulder, other hands "held," but not the kind of full-body-contact slow dances I remember from high school. I do recall stories of some kissing occurring during these dances, but that never happened to me.

Our last football game of the season was held at a field near the beach. It was really cold that day, with a bitter wind blowing off the water. It even looks cold in the grainy black and white photos I have in my box of St. Felicitas memorabilia. Despite the cold, we girls were there, cheering on the team. Football season ended with a banquet in those infamous green rooms in the church basement. Not long after, it was the season for midnight mass, where we eighth graders again had the leading roles. If a romance that had sparked in a basement at a football party lasted until Christmas, gifts might be discreetly exchanged, but most of the gift-giving happened within families. Our Christmas lists, which had replaced letters to Santa years ago, contained a few items of clothing but mostly we wanted records, those infamous little 45s that made the careers of our musical heroes. We loved the pop songs that were everywhere that year—Lulu's "To Sir with Love" and The Monkees' "Daydream Believer," in addition to the latest Beatles hits—but we also loved Motown—Martha and the Vandellas' "Jimmy Mack," Marvin Gaye's "I Heard it Through the Grapevine" and, of course, Aretha Franklin's "Respect." It was a great era for music.

We girls would walk from house to house, carrying those little 45rpm records to play on each other's turntables. Our clique was all white girls, but, when we had parties, they were open to everyone, and many of our black classmates attended. Beth remembers a time when we were walking down a block with black teenagers walking near us, and one of our friends said (to us not to them), "They would want the music that I'm carrying around. It's their music." We did love those Motown artists. Sheila recalled a dance in the green rooms with another South Side Catholic school. One of our black classmates, Katie, complimented her on her dance moves. Sheila was friendly with Katie and felt that Katie liked her. She was pleased that Katie admired her dancing. Music was great for bringing us together.

Inside our school, black and white kids still generally got along, we were able to have fun and make each other laugh, typical teenagers. The guys got along well enough to have really good sports teams; they seemed to enjoy playing sports together. Thomas Mills was one of the black students who had joined our class in seventh grade. He was already over six feet tall. After some excellent coaching, he became very good at playing basketball – making him a school hero. A few of the black girls had joined us as cheerleaders, especially those who had been in our school for several years by then.

I remember one day after school, a group of both black and white kids from St. Felicitas were hanging out near the Little Del. I don't recall everyone who was there, but Katie definitely was. Everybody liked Katie and she was friendly with the white girls. She went to the same high school I attended as a freshman, before I moved away. Katie went there all four years and was president of her senior class. She was always a leader. This particular day, we were engaged in a playful shouting match—the black kids were yelling "Black Power" and the white kids shouted back "White Power." I think the reason I remember this so clearly is that it felt wrong to me at first, maybe even dangerous, but it was all in good fun, everyone ended up just laughing. I'd like to think that, at fourteen, we were making fun of a social and political movement because it made no sense to us, but I don't think we were that enlightened.

Tension

Although we never really "hung out" with the black girls in our class, we would greet them and maybe stop and talk for a few minutes if we saw them outside of school. By eighth grade, however, there would be times when they were with their black friends, kids that didn't go to our school, and they wouldn't always stop to chat—or even acknowledge that they knew us. It wasn't a major thing, but it felt weird and we were unsure how to react. Those other kids, the ones from the public schools, or from outside our neighborhood, were the ones we had learned to fear.

Beth remembers a day when she was babysitting, right across the street from our church. All of a sudden, she heard a ruckus outside. She looked out and saw a bunch of black guys and a bunch of white guys fighting. It wasn't anyone she recognized; they didn't go to our school. The police came and the kids ran through the gangway between the house where Beth was and the house next door. She knew they were hiding in the backyard and she recalls how frightened she was, despite how close the house was to our normally safe school and church.

Occasionally, we did have confrontations with our classmates. Sheila recalls getting into a fight with Paula Wilson. Paula came up behind Sheila right outside of school and hit her. You might recall that Paula had terrorized my friend Eileen a couple of years earlier. Like the rest of us, Sheila had never been in a fight and didn't fight back. She does remember, with regret, that she called Paula "the 'n' word." She felt terrible and remembers that transgression more than being beaten up. She knew it was wrong to use that word, no matter what the girl was doing to her. Her parents taught her: "Don't judge, you never know what a person is going through."

The incidents of violence were now increasing. Eileen remembers a time she was looking out the front window of her house, watching her dad and brother walking their dog. She saw a friend of her brother's getting beaten up by a bunch of black guys, just two houses away, right on the front sidewalk. Her dad saw it, too, and just let the dog go, off the leash. Their dog did not like black people; they had to use a chain to hold her because she could break a leather leash. When Eileen's dad let go of the chain, the dog headed for the kids that were attacking her brother's friend. They took off. They did not like the dog any more than the dog liked them.

It was not just white families that were starting to be concerned about the neighborhood. The young black couple that lived next door to us sent their children to their grandparents in Mississippi to attend school. They feared their son would be recruited by the youth gangs that had begun forming on the South Side of Chicago. Recruiting by gangs was aggressive and often happened inside public high schools, sometimes resulting in violence.[5]

Basketball

Basketball season brought another chance at glory for the boy athletes and girl cheerleaders of St. Felicitas. Since gyms are smaller than football fields, there were fewer players and cheerers, so many of us were relegated to the bleachers. I was one of those, but I still have great memories of the sport. Our gym, the old converted church, was not big enough for bleachers, so there were no home games. This complicated our ability to attend, but we certainly tried. My parents had two cars and only three children, so they were often the ones who drove us. (Most families in the parish had one car and six or more children.) Our team was the best the school had seen in several years. They were aided by our excellent coaches, who were just a few years older than the team. Having Thomas Mills at center also gave us some advantage; he was several inches taller than most eighth graders.

We made it to the championship game of the city-wide Catholic Youth Organization (CYO), where we played an all-white team from the northern suburbs on St. Patrick's Day. Despite our tall center, the rest of our team was significantly shorter than their opponents. The opposing school was also much bigger than ours, and, based on its location on the more prosperous North Side, probably had more money, which may have bought them some advantage. Whatever the reason, we were clearly underdogs in the match up.

I remember the details of this game because I chose it as the topic of an essay I wrote that school year. I still have the essay, neatly handwritten on three-hole-punch ruled paper with front and back covers of construction paper carefully stapled (twice) at the top left corner. The back cover is red, and the front is white, though faded. On the cover I have glued a cut-out from the actual program from the game (which I also still have)—a jumping basketball player sketch, attributed to someone named Don Toole. In red magic marker, traced over pencil, is written my title for the piece: "the BIG GAME." I must have turned this in for extra credit, as it does not show any teacher's red ink and is not graded. If it had been a mandatory assignment, there would surely have been some markings. Its pristine condition is probably why I have kept it for fifty years and moved it with my possessions at least fifteen times. Below is the essay, written by me at fourteen, in its entirety. I have retained the punctuation and spelling errors but corrected my tendency to split words at odd places, which would be quite distracting, especially now that word processors have all but eliminated word division at the end of lines.

The Big Game – written by me in 8th grade, 1968:

Excitement began to build as the crowd was gathering on the St. Felicitas school grounds. There were adults there to drive, girls there to cheer, and a jam-packed busload of sixth through eighth graders ready and willing to cheer along with them in a desperate attempt to win.

That was the scene on March seventeenth at one p.m. We would soon be on our way to the Gordon Tech gym for the CYO basketball city championship game. This was to be the last game of a victorious season and everyone had crossed their fingers and said a prayer that the class of '68 would end its season with the most important 1st place trophy.

As the bus prepared to leave, I watched the cars carrying our top-notch team and coaches as they pulled out of the lot. With pride in our hearts we gave them our peppiest cheer accompanied by cries of "good luck" and "we've gotta win, we've gotta win."

There were very few minutes or even seconds of quiet as Mr. King, our bus driver made his way through expressway after expressway of Sunday traffic on our cross-city venture of forty-five minutes. But the noise began to diminish as he pulled chartered bus no. 233 into the parking lot of a new and modern high school building.

No one knew quite where to go or what to do but a feeling of togetherness spread through the crowd as we knew we were all there for one specific purpose: to support the No. 1 south-side team as they met the famed suburban St. John Brebeuf's.

I entered a beautiful large gym just before half in the game for 3rd place. With anticipation and quite a lot of fear for the unknown I took a seat in the grandstand-like bleachers where our team and those members of the parish who had come by car were already impatiently waiting out the clock for our game to begin.

At two-fifteen our team took the court. After a five minute practice they were given a short time to go over plays with the coaches. A voice came over the loud speaker welcoming the spectators, announcing the situation, and lastly introducing the teams. First St. John Brebeuf's first-stringers took their places on the center of the court. The announcer's voice accompanied by an overflowment of cheers, applause, and shouts of encouragement from the stands then brought the Fantastic Felicitas Five to the floor. Handshakes were given, accepted, and the players finally took their positions.

St. John's took the ball on the tip-off as the clock began to run. Before I knew what had happened, someone called time out, and Brebeuf's had the lead. The St. John's crowd began to stir with excitement. ___. No one around me moved; we all sat stone-still and waited for the game to reopen.

At the next time out Felicitas had tied it 12-12. The gaity and pep of the Felicitas crowd were restored, as we began to stir again with pride. Our team wasn't going to be beaten that easily.

But, although the Falcon's took the next tip and scored a basket, it seemed to me that their points were outnumber two-to-one by St. John's. Because of my limited knowledge of basketball, I just couldn't figure out why this was so. Listening to the huge man seated behind me in his St. Patrick's Day green sweater, I learned that the Falcon's ". . . just aren't (weren't) getting those rebounds!" I accepted this as a good enough reason for the score – since I didn't know of any better. By half it rested 20-14 in favor of St. John's.

Half time provided a break in the tension for all except the coaches and four of the eighth grade girls. These girls are the four cheerleaders who then had to face going out in front of a vast crowd and performing such feats as a cartwheel, the splits, and their perfected end-of-cheer jump. They all seemed to be scared stiff, but every ounce of fear seemed to have drained from them by the time they reached the center of the gym, for they gave a splendid performance illustrating the true St. Felicitas spirit.

The second half seemed to start out as a direct rerun of the first. Thrilling plays were contributed by both sides, but once again St. John's overwhelming skill seemed to bring about most of the highlights. Scoring again went on at both baskets as each team more than doubled its half-time score.

For the last few minutes of the game, which in basketball is more like a few centuries, the second string was put in to play __, for the team knew that they had been beaten. Sure enough, the game slowly drew to a close: 41–26 St. John Brebeuf's were City Champs!

For the first few minutes after the game it was hard for me to let all this sink in, but it was really obvious from the very way that the game had progressed. Although our school had a really great team (the best since 1963) they had been matched to one of even more skill and understanding of the game.

If I have ever felt disappointment it was right then and I imagine that those around me felt it also.

Then I was watching the team receive their 2nd place trophies and thinking of how much more depressed they must be than me. The other girls around me must have sensed this also because we came out with the liveliest cheers for the team that we had had all day, and by the time we left the gym and piled again into our bus I am sure that each and every one had decided in himself that the second place team still rated an honorable place on top to us. We had come in number 2 and that was great enough, after all some team somewhere had come in number 177!

Funny, all these years later, if you had asked me, I would have said we won. The memory is a positive one, despite the outcome. Or maybe it just feels positive, since our world was about to take a major turn for the worse.

Two weeks later, on March 31st, 1968, President Johnson came on television to tell us he would not run for re-election. He had accomplished much in support of the Civil Rights Movement, but the Vietnam War had done him in. The Tet Offensive, earlier that year, had turned the mood of the country decidedly against the war. The Mai Lai Massacre happened around this time also, although the public didn't hear about it for over a year. I don't know when LBJ heard about it. I'm sure he heard the protesters, though, who had gotten personal with their slogan, "Hey, hey, LBJ, how many kids did you kill today?"

My biggest worry after that big game was getting my dress finished for the basketball banquet. Going all the way to city championship for the CYO was much to celebrate indeed. At fourteen, most girls, myself included, thought that what they wore to a big event like this was of the utmost importance. It needed to be something new, special and not like everyone else – but really, not too different, either. I wasn't allowed to take sewing classes at the park anymore, it was too dangerous there, but I could always get help from my mother who was an excellent seamstress. Using my precious after-school time, reserved for hanging out with my friends, was a big sacrifice, but I needed that dress, so I was willing to make it. I wore the dress in my class photo that year, too, but I would remember it even if I did not have that evidence. It was pumpkin-colored wool with long sleeves and lots of stitching down the front. It was a lot of work to get it done in time.

Then, the unthinkable happened. The banquet was cancelled. I was crushed; my world was in crisis. My friends were in tears. Why did the adults make such a terrible decision? How could such tragedy strike us at this critical point in our lives? The banquet was scheduled for April 5, 1968.

The King Assassination

The Reverend Dr. Martin Luther King, Jr. was shot and killed the evening of April 4, 1968 in Memphis, Tennessee. We went to school the next day anyway, not realizing what was about to happen. Around noon, our school went on lockdown. I don't think we had a word for it then; it had never happened before. Everyone was moved from their individual classrooms into the church next door, and parents had to pick their children up there. No one was allowed to walk home without an adult. Something big was happening. Everyone was on edge.

The nearest business district to our school was 87th Street near Stony Island. Chicago Vocational School (CVS), the nearest public high school, was on the same street, a bit further east. Beth, who lived near CVS, remembers big groups of black teenagers streaming out of the school, walking ten abreast down 87th Street, breaking store windows. The family of one of our classmates owned a hardware store there, and word spread that his dad stood in front of it that afternoon with a shotgun. We had never heard of anyone having a shotgun. His windows were probably the only ones not broken on 87th Street that day. As far as I know, he didn't fire a shot.

That afternoon was terrifying for Beth and other kids who lived on the southern end of our neighborhood, near CVS high school. They were in their homes with their siblings and mothers, while people were running up and down the gangways between the houses. Those gangways were only about five-feet wide; it felt very close. Kids were afraid the rioters would break into their homes. Who knows what might happen then? Fathers, who were our protectors, were still at work. This all happened very fast. The police managed to get the teenagers off the streets near us shortly after dark. Other parts of the city were not so lucky, as we would soon learn.

Laura heard from her brothers that the leaders of the Blackstone Rangers street gang offered to protect Mt. Carmel, the boys' Catholic high school in the heart of their territory, on that fear-filled day. Many boys from St. Felicitas parish were in school there, including my sister Terry's boyfriend. Eileen heard a different story—the gang was going to burn the school down until the priests talked them out of it. A student who was at Mt. Carmel that day told me that the leader of the Blackstone Rangers ordered gang members to break the arms of one of his deputies who wanted to attack the school. In addition to these antidotes, I found three different published versions of what happened at Mt. Carmel that day. In one, a local minister who allowed the gang to meet at his church convinced the gang that rioting would just hurt their own neighborhood.[5] Another describes a harrowing scene in which a mob of students from a public high school formed to attack Mt. Carmel, but the leader of the Blackstone Rangers "immediately understood" that it would be a bad idea to attack the school and stopped the mob with force. The gang then saluted each bus of Mt. Carmel students as they left the school property.[6] The third version of the story also describes the high school mob but credits the police for stopping them. It goes on to say that the Blackstone Rangers rocked the buses of Mt. Carmel students as they left the property and yelled "Blackstone!" at them—the chant they often used to demonstrate their authority over the neighborhood.[7] Regardless of what actually happened at Mt. Carmel that day, most published accounts of that weekend conclude that the gang helped to keep the peace in their South Side neighborhood—or at least didn't cause any rioting of their own.

That night there was no St. Felicitas basketball banquet, but there were riots—in parts of Chicago and in many cities and towns around the country. On the West Side of Chicago, two miles of buildings were destroyed by fire. Afterward, Mayor Daley famously issued a "shoot to kill" order for arsonists and "shoot to main" for looters.[8] The National Guard was called in, and many areas were blockaded to prevent further violence and looting. Parts of the city, some within a couple of miles of my house, were essentially turned into a police state. By the end of the weekend, nine people had died, hundreds were injured and over 162 buildings had been destroyed by arson. And that was just in Chicago.[9]

The normal curfew for teenagers was moved up from 10 o'clock to 6 o'clock for the next few weeks. No one under 18 could go out at night, unless you had a ride. My friends and I never walked around after dark, so this didn't really affect us, but my sister Terry's boyfriend couldn't come to visit her after dinner, which she considered a catastrophe. Some nights my parents drove him—to keep the peace inside our house.

Looking back, I believe that the riots that followed Reverend King's assassination were what led many parents of St. Felicitas kids to realize they could no longer keep us safe in our neighborhood. It seems to have been a turning point in their attempt to live in an integrated community. I don't recall ever discussing that day or the assassination with my black classmates, and don't remember the teachers dealing with it when we returned to school, but things were decidedly different in our world afterward. The level of tension went up and stayed up.

In case you are concerned, we had our basketball banquet later that month. I wore the dress. Teenage life still went on.

Trouble on Stony Island

Stony Island Boulevard was one of the primary commercial areas in our neighborhood. We were on Stony often because our favorite neighborhood hangouts, the Little Del and the instrument building, were there, as well as the all-important bakery we still visited before mass each school day. The variety of other businesses along Stony made walking there more interesting than walking on the residential streets. There was at least one funeral home. I don't recall its name but remember my friends and I stopping in when we were in the sixth grade to visit with a classmate who lost her mother. This must have been the idea of one of our mothers; they were probably more freaked out by the girl losing her mom than we were. During our years at St. Felicitas, we would go there to attend wakes for three of our classmates, as well as Fathers Kelley and O'Donnell. Many sad memories in that place.

Farther down Stony there was a hotel, the Zanzibar, which was just a generic 1960s motel, but sounded exotic to us. Along the way were several eating establishments: a walk-up Tastee Freeze ice cream stand; our neighborhood hamburger joint, named Super Burger; Wee Mac's, a diner with table service, where my family sometime went after church on Sundays; and a fast food chicken place that opened in the later years—counter service only, no drive-throughs back then. Stony Island played a big role in our neighborhood and it was a thriving commercial area in the 1960s.

The "trouble" on Stony Island began with the infamous coke bottle incident. This one was elevated to the status of a neighborhood legend. Everyone knew about it. I think I saw it happen but can't be sure. The story was so often repeated that everyone felt as if they had been there. The star of the show was Gloria Davis. Gloria didn't attend our school but was often seen around the neighborhood and usually had group of black kids with her, an entourage of sorts, but not the good kind. Gloria always seemed to be mad, and she was particularly mad at one of my classmates, David. I don't think he had done anything to her, but he didn't let her scare him and had probably engaged in verbal conflict with her and her friends from time to time. My friend Sheila was David's girlfriend. Sheila felt unsafe because Gloria would say things to her and be threatening toward her, just because she was David's girlfriend. Gloria was the worst example of the bullying black girls who confronted us. We were more afraid of those black girls than of any of the boys, because they showed contempt toward us and were willing to fight at the drop of a hat. They knew how to fight; they could hurt you. Those girls were willing to fight boys, too, white boys.

Word had spread through the neighborhood that Gloria was after David. She was going to get him, and she was going to get Sheila. Sheila and I lived near each other, so we often walked places together. If we saw Gloria coming towards us, we went the opposite direction. We girls never traveled alone now, at least two of us would be together, often five or six. If there was a group of black kids coming towards us, we would have to get off the sidewalk. We had to step aside, or they'd become belligerent. It wasn't like they would step to one side and we would step to the other. No, they barged right through, even knocking some of us out of their way if we didn't move quickly enough. It felt to us like a kind of bravado, like they were saying: "We are going to show you."

When Sheila and I saw a group coming towards us, we were always wondering if it might be Gloria and her friends, or someone else who would taunt us or chase us. All of these situations could lead to confrontations that we did not know how to handle. We were fourteen years old; although we were fearful, we didn't really recognize the extent of the danger we might be facing. We hid things from our parents and teachers, because they would just add more limits on where we could go and what we could do if they knew what was happening to us. A few of us "armed" ourselves. I often carried an empty pop bottle with me, and Beth carried a dog's choke chain, concealed inside the lining of her coat. I can't imagine us ever using these weapons, but somehow, they made us feel a little safer. I do know that I got really good at screaming loudly and running fast. Sometimes that was enough to end the potential, or imagined, confrontation. There were always adults somewhere nearby that might come out and see what was happening. Even the bullying entourage of Gloria Davis would have respect for adults, or so we hoped.

One day Sheila and David were at the Little Del. It was full of kids, as always. This time Gloria was there. David said something that provoked her. He had just finished a bottle of pop and he handed it to her, saying "Here's two cents," implying that was about what she was worth. (Pop bottles could be returned for a two-cent deposit back then.) He definitely wasn't being nice by giving her the bottle. Gloria grabbed the bottle from him. As David was walking away from her, she cracked him over the back of his head with it. Right there in the store. The bottle broke and glass fell everywhere. Sheila remembers that David looked stunned at first—then fell to the ground. Those old coke bottles were made of thick glass.

This was no joke. It was assault. David had antagonized Gloria, but she had thrown the first "punch." The owner of the Little Del surely called the police, and we heard that the cops had talked to Gloria about it; she was already on their radar. I don't know if this would have gotten her into juvenile detention at that time, but it was one of the worst incidents we girls had witnessed, and it probably played a part in David's family deciding to move away.

Gloria also figures prominently in a story that one of the Groundsmen, Alan, told me. Alan and a friend from a nearby parish were hanging out at the "grounds," as usual, when Alan's older brother arrived with his friend, a linebacker for his high school football team. A group of about twenty-five black teenagers came walking toward the four boys from the direction of Stony Island. Some of the black kids were carrying clubs, chains and boards with whips attached to them. As they approached and circled the four boys, a girl stepped forward from the group and said: "My name is Gloria Davis. I am from Harlem, New York, and I am the meanest (expletive) bitch you have ever seen." The black youths began to ask Alan and his friends if they were Groundsmen. When one of them answered yes, he was lashed with one of the whips by a black youth. During the scuffle that followed, Alan walked slowly away and crossed the street toward the school janitor's house. The other boys thought Alan had deserted them. He walked quickly by the house and through the yard to the garage where the Groundsmen kept a cache of weapons, hidden behind the fence. Their "weapons" consisted of bottles and bats. Alan grabbed a box of bottles and came running out toward the playground. He started throwing bottles at the black youths and yelling expletives at them.

A serious fight was now in progress. One of the Groundsmen was able to get a club away from one of the black youths. He used it to defend himself when he was struck by a six-foot chain. He ended up with welts across his chest and back; his attacker was left bleeding seriously from his head. The Groundsmen started backing away, until they saw another group of ten blacks coming toward them, kids from the public school. Their only escape route was now blocked; they were badly outnumbered and surrounded. Luckily, as their supply of bottles began to run out, the neighborhood youth officer arrived by car and called the police on his two-way radio. Just then, another Groundsman came by in a car, and the four boys were able to jump in and drive away. They went to a neighboring parish's school grounds, where they still felt safe.

I was quite surprised to learn that a few of my eighth-grade classmates were arrested that April. I heard about it while researching this book and was able to find an article in "The Daily Defender" to support it. "The Daily Defender" is a long-standing African-American newspaper in Chicago. I believe it is considered a reputable publication, but the title of the story sounds biased to me. It insinuates that my classmates were "nabbed" for an attack on the home of a black family. That is not what they were stopped for, as the rest of the article makes clear. I admit that I have my own biases as I read this article now. I am also appalled that they listed the names and addresses of the boys, who were clearly minors, all between thirteen and sixteen years old. They even mention that one of them is the son and brother of Chicago cops. Sounds like a good way to make these young boys targets of retaliation.

According to the article, a "fire bomb," (a rag saturated with something flammable and tied around a board), was thrown through the window of the home of a black newspaper reporter and his wife, who had been labeled a troublemaker by another paper, the white-controlled "Daily Calumet." She and her husband were actively involved in neighborhood groups; their home had been attacked before. Their twelve-year-old son, who was the only one home at the time of this attack, told police he saw a young white man running away after it happened, but could not identify him. While a police officer was in the neighborhood writing up his report of the crime, he saw a group of five white boys discard a knife and a toy pop-gun. The boys, two of them my classmates, were arrested for illegal possession of a weapon, not for the attack on the home. The homeowners' sixteen-year-old son told the reporter that he saw these same boys throw two empty motor oil cans into the driveway of a building near his house earlier that day. He said that he had told the police about it. This key fact was not in the police report, according to the paper. I've had more than one source tell me that reports of the Chicago police department were not always reliable at that time, so I really can't say whose side to believe in this case.

Clearly, the five white teenagers were up to some mischief, but there doesn't seem to be evidence that actually tied them to this firebombing. From the addresses listed in the paper, I can tell that at least some of the boys lived near the attacked house, so their proximity to the crime does not seem suspicious. At the end of the article, the reporter chose to mention that "Negro parents in the area say that black youngsters are being harassed by members of two white youth gangs known as the Vandals and the Imperial Guardsmen." She then adds: "It was not known whether the white youths arrested are members of either gang." I had no idea that this had happened and, as far as I know, the two boys from my class finished eighth grade and graduated with us. If they belonged to a "gang," it was probably that non-gang gang, the Groundsmen.

One day, Eileen, Beth, Laura and Sheila were walking on Stony, minding their own business, when they saw a group of black girls walking towards them. It was not long after Reverend King's assassination; things were still volatile all over the city. It was probably not a good idea for any of us to be out yet, but we were still a little defiant. It was our neighborhood and we felt we should be able to walk around in it. They were probably just walking to Beth's house after a visit to the Del. When they saw the black girls, they crossed all six lanes of Stony and its wide median to the other side of the street, as had become our habit. But the black girls also crossed and approached them. They were talking loudly and saying things to intimidate the white girls, who were trying to ignore them. We never intentionally started any trouble; we were mostly just busy trying to stay out of it. Then Gloria Davis breaks through the group, points to Beth and proceeds to slap her in the face. The "flight" instinct kicked in but, as the white girls were running away, Gloria's group gave chase. Someone got hold of a winter scarf around Eileen's neck and pulled it, choking her. Eileen broke free, but Gloria then caught up with Laura, the smallest girl in our group. She grabbed Laura's coat and pulled her, spinning her around as she tried to scream. This infuriated Beth, who was a pretty brave girl and bigger than Gloria, who Beth describes as "a little scrappy thing." She couldn't just let her friend get attacked. She was able to pull Laura away—then she surprised everyone by punching Gloria Davis. Beth and Laura took advantage of the element of surprise and took off, slapping high fives to each other as they ran, trying to catch up with Eileen and Sheila. The black girls did not chase them very far after that, but they kept running until they were safe at Beth's house, where at least some of her siblings and probably one or both parents would be home. All of the girls, and the rest of us, were now terrified that the "trouble" had become physical.

None of us walked around the neighborhood alone anymore; now we were even leery about walking in groups. We did still go to the Little Del, though, it was only half a block from school, and we needed our cokes and chips. One day as we were on our way there, we heard that Gloria was in the store. Fearing that Gloria was still after her, Sheila turned around and headed straight home. As the rest of us approached the store, a black teenager who we didn't know began walking towards Beth, staring her down. Beth kept looking right at him, right in his face, trying to be cool and appear tough. She was scared but not enough to back away. After all, we were right in front of the Del and there were plenty of people around. As he got close, he spit, right in Beth's face. She assumed Gloria told him to do it—to retaliate for the punching incident. He said, "Sorry, I thought you were someone else," and Beth responded, "That's okay," wiping her face with the back of her hand and continuing to walk toward the store. She wasn't going to fight him, that wasn't something we did. The only reason she hit Gloria was to get her to let go of Laura. And she ran away after that. If it was fight or flight, we always chose flight.

These kinds of events just became part of our everyday reality, sometime around eighth grade. We started to feel that we were being hunted. We still walked home from school, but eventually the Del became another place, like the park, we just didn't go as often, because we were afraid of what might happen to us there. It wasn't safe to be on Stony Island anymore; that was for sure. We couldn't wander the neighborhood in the same way we once had. Our life was changing, being restricted, at an age when most young people are gaining more freedom.

At the same time our parents were restricting our activities, they were encouraging us to be tolerant. Laura's parents taught her and her siblings to:

> ". . . have a sense of compassion for, well, for everybody. They really believed in helping the person out who is less fortunate. In my home you were never going to use the 'n' word. We were going to accept the change in the neighborhood and live with it and see . . . we're going to see where this takes us."

Eileen remembers a day when she was hanging her coat up in the cloakroom next to our classroom and Katie, one of our black classmates, told her that there was a plan to "burn down Marynook," where Eileen lived. She was warning Eileen, out of friendship, to get out of there. No attempt was ever made to burn Marynook, as far as we know, but Eileen was glad that Katie cared enough about her to warn her that it might.

May Procession

The "trouble" did not stop our parish traditions. One of our most cherished events was the May Procession. As part of the build up to it, the eighth-grade girls would choose a May Queen and her court—girls who got to dress up and bring up the rear of the procession—the stars of the show. Somehow, despite the lesson the nuns tried to teach us during cheerleader picking, my friends and I thought we were still in control of the social scene at St. Felicitas. Picking the May Queen seemed well within our domain. We knew, of course, it would be one of "us." This was the crowning glory of eighth grade. The only time that one, and only one, girl was in the spotlight. To us, it was the equivalent of being homecoming queen in high school, with similar fanfare and glory. All of the St. Felicitas students marched in the procession, and every parish member watched it. For that matter, most everyone who lived in the neighborhood watched it. How could they miss that many kids walking down the middle of the street? The spotlight was huge. The queen's court were the runners up in the very democratic, (or so we thought), election process. The queen and her court wore formal attire, most likely their older sisters' prom dresses, but possibly something bought, or more likely sewn, just for them. The rest of the eighth-grade girls wore their uniforms, just as we all had most every year. Eighth graders did get to adorn their uniforms with graduation ribbons, but that was not anything like the special status of being the queen or one of her attendants.

The totally-fair election process went like this: we, defined as those girls who had been picked as cheerleaders in seventh grade, (we didn't know the word clique, but that's what we were), each wrote a name on a secret ballot. The ballots were tallied. She who got the most votes was elected May Queen. The next highest vote getters were her attendants. There were only about a dozen of us, so this did not take very long. The voting took place in the back of a classroom, after school was over for the day. Beth was in charge of counting the votes, since she was good at math. As we anxiously awaited the results, Sister Marciana happened upon us. Once again, we got that look that made you feel that you had disappointed God and all of the saints and apostles at once. This year, we were informed, every eighth-grade girl would have an equal chance of being queen. To be sure it was equal, the names would be drawn out of a hat. There were about 30 girls in our class, so this really changed the odds of one of "us" winning. But we still had a chance.

I wonder now if we really did have a chance. I would not become an auditor until many years later, but now I have a sneaky feeling that this lottery was fixed. To our disbelief, not only was the winner not one of us, it was Martha Edwards—the same Martha Edwards who had bullied Laura and who had not even chosen to be a cheerleader when she had the chance. She was one of those bullies who were big for their age, or at least bigger than most of us—and black. A black May Queen? Surely there was a rule against that. The queen was actually representing Mary, mother of Jesus, who we were absolutely sure was white. We did not protest, however. That was not our style. We had never challenged the authority of our parents, and certainly not that of the nuns. We retreated to my basement and commiserated; tears were shed. Eighth grade was all but destroyed, and we still had over a month to go until graduation.

Sheila remembers an incident related to the procession involving another one of our black classmates, Lisa Stevens. Everyone really liked Lisa; she hosted a party at her house that year and several of us went. We might actually have been a little less upset if she had been the May Queen, instead of Martha. Lisa was picked as part of the entourage that got to wear long dresses, but she was absent that day. The nuns decided there was a need to practice the pageantry that very day, so they couldn't wait for Lisa. They asked if anyone else had a long dress, and Sheila jumped right in. She had nothing against Lisa; she just wanted to be part of the queen's court. She had three older sisters, so coming up with a second-hand prom dress would not be a problem. When Lisa came back to school, she gave Sheila a hard time about it. Sheila felt that Lisa was trying to make it into a racial incident, when it wasn't. Luckily, this incident was isolated. Lisa went to my high school, and I remember her as friendly.

On the day of the May Procession, our queen appeared in a full-length wedding gown. We thought her parents must have been a little crazy to invest in a wedding dress for a fourteen-year-old, or maybe they just had more money than any of our parents, or both. The dress really seemed over the top, tacky even, to us—confirmation that she was not worthy of the honor which had been bestowed upon her. One of us would have made a more tasteful choice. But we marched along in front of her, leading her through the neighborhood and into the church, just as if this was a normal May Procession, because that was how we behaved.

Looking back now, I realize that the dress, whether it actually was a wedding dress or not, meant that being May Queen was a really big deal for Martha and her family. Why *shouldn't* she have the same opportunity to shine as those of us who had attended St. Felicitas all nine years? It was her eighth-grade year, too. Looking at photos from that time, I realize now that Martha was also a very pretty girl and looked spectacular in the dress. If only I had been a little more enlightened, and less self-centered, at fourteen, I might have even complimented her that day. Now I wish I had.

Graduation

Even as the world seemed to be falling apart around us, with violence literally in the streets, and our reign as top dogs seriously undermined, we were looking forward to the next big event—graduation—with all its related festivities. Our class was treated to field trips to Brookfield Zoo and an amusement park, a breakfast in our honor, and a party in the good old green rooms, complete with a live band. That was not the only party, though. The night after graduation, when we had finished celebrating with our families, we went "house hopping." This meant a series of short parties at the home of any classmate whose parents were open to the idea of dozens of teenagers dropping by for twenty minutes or so. The partying didn't end there, either. A series of full-length parties started right after graduation and lasted pretty much all summer, until we ran out of houses with willing parents. Similar to football parties, most graduation parties were held in our basements with plenty of records on the turntable.

Graduation itself took place at the church, late on a Thursday afternoon in June. Although it wasn't a religious ceremony, the church was really the only place big enough for the graduates (there were nearly 80 of us) and all our well-wishers. Just like we had for First Communion and Confirmation, we practiced marching two by two from the school to the church, where we would sit quietly in the pews, until it was our turn to go to the front. It looked like every other graduation I have been to, except that there was an altar. We walked across in front of it and were handed our diplomas by Monsignor Walsh. Our graduation gowns were blue, and the tassels on our mortar boards were gold. For some reason our "academic" school colors were different from our school sports colors of red and white. My guess is that the gowns had been donated from another school. The gowns were shared year to year and replacing them would have been beyond the resources of the school and most of the families in the parish. At least they were made of real material, not the triple polyester of the current, throw-away versions.

We were understandably excited that we were about to participate in this, the ultimate milestone of St. Felicitas School, when tragedy struck the nation once again. In the early morning hours of our graduation day, Bobby Kennedy was shot in Los Angeles, after winning the California primary the night before. He had been the frontrunner for the Democratic nomination for president. He died the following morning. Another prominent Irish Catholic removed from the leadership of our country. Although tragic, his death wasn't followed by riots, and our graduation ceremony was allowed to be held that evening as planned.

Summer of '68

I had a graduation party at my house that summer. Our house had the very best basement. Most basements in the neighborhood (except those in Marynook) were more or less unfinished, with concrete floors and walls. My parents had ours renovated in the early sixties. We had wood paneling on our walls, a linoleum floor that included a "tiled in" shuffleboard court and a pool table that would need to be covered and moved out of the way for dancing at the party. A wooden bar covered one full wall, but, instead of liquor, its main feature was a functioning Coke machine, a perk of my dad being in the grocery business. Food was limited to chips and dip, but the Coca-Cola was flowing. Stacks of 45rpm records would play over and over. Everyone brought records to the parties; no one could possibly have all the hits we loved in their personal collection. To keep them straight, we wrote our names on the labels. Like football parties, fast dances were mostly done by girls in groups, but the highlight was those slow dances.

My parents liked to tell about Thomas Mills arriving at my party. He was the six-foot-three-inch basketball center. Tom lived just down the street from us, so he arrived alone instead of with a group; other kids walked from their blocks together. He came in the front door because he had never been in our house before. Those in the know came in the back door, right next to the stairs to the basement. I don't know who opened the door for Thomas, but he didn't know which way to head—and ended up in the living room face to face with my parents. They said he looked startled, and they were startled, too. Despite our many black neighbors and classmates, it was unusual to have such a tall, skinny black teenager wander into the living room. They tried to make him feel welcome, and showed him the way to the basement, where he joined the rest of the class for my party.

We also had a door directly into the basement that was rarely ever used. James Malone showed up at that door, which should have been a clue he was up to no good. I let him in, undoubtedly breaking a house rule, and he showed me something he had in his pocket. I had no idea what it was. He told me it was "weed," which I had barely heard of and had certainly never seen. This was definitely breaking rules, and laws, which made me very nervous, but I was still a fourteen-year-old girl and wasn't about to run tell my parents or ask him to leave. I wasn't even sure it was really weed. I have no idea what became of it, but surely would have noticed if someone was smoking in my basement, smoking anything.

Although he was still Sheila's boyfriend, David asked me to dance that night. Sheila wasn't jealous; this was a tradition of David's. If the party was at a girl's house, he would ask that girl to dance as a way of thanking her for having the party. We thought that was pretty polite for boys in our class. David obviously had older sisters.

One very special party that summer was held at a fancy hotel close to downtown. The father of one of our classmates was the owner of the restaurant in the hotel. Consequently, this party featured much better food than what we were used to—which wasn't difficult since we were mostly served potato chips at other parties. Her dad hired a live band for us too; no need to bring our 45s. What I remember most clearly about this party was that David bought Sheila a corsage to wear—an orchid, no less. This was also something atypical of boys our age. Maybe David really was special, or at least more thoughtful, than most boys, sisters or not.

That summer was not all about parties, by any means. Having turned fourteen that spring, I insisted that my father live up to a promise he made that I could work in his grocery store starting that year—and earn my own money. I had been paid for cleaning shelves in the store during a few summer vacations, but that was not steady work. I wanted to wear a uniform and check out groceries on a regular basis, earning a paycheck to buy my own records and other important items, like clothes. Not that I was deprived; heaven knows our family had more than most, and I don't remember ever being told we could not afford something. But I inherited my father's work ethic and I wanted to earn my own way—or at least my own totally unnecessary stuff. So, he put me on the payroll at $1.25 an hour. That was below the minimum wage of $1.60, but I guess, given my being under the typical first-year-of-working age (16) and the fact that my mother had to drive me, he felt my work should be discounted.

According to my official record with the Social Security Administration, I earned $425 in 1968 and another $670 before we moved in 1969—which calculates to close to 900 hours at that cash register. I got pretty good at it. I can still tell you the price of our most common sale: a loaf of bread and a half gallon of milk ($1.02). Prices were marked on most items, but it was faster to just memorize them. Scanners were not even imagined at that time. I almost always had someone else at the checkout area with me, probably because my parents were worried that I was a bit too vulnerable up there alone. It was a small store, compared to the ones we have today, with just two checkout counters. Only one was normally in use. The checkout was, of course, right at the front door, in a neighborhood only marginally safer than the one where we lived. It was a busy place and street, though, so I never felt unsafe. I have a clear memory of a teenager (I think he was someone I knew) coming in to the store one day yelling, "We finally beat the Commies!" It was the day that Apollo 8 orbited the moon.

Meanwhile, the danger in the neighborhood where we lived continued to escalate. Beth remembers two instances near her house when somebody came through shooting BB guns. They shot her two brothers, a younger brother, who was pretty small at the time, and an older brother, who went after them.

> "They were in a car—it was a 'drive-by' shooting, but with BBs. So, my little brother was shot. But you know, BBs, they hurt, but they don't kill you. I still remember my other brother chasing after the shooter, and he was getting shot. And I still remember it clearly; it was kind of like a movie. He was getting shot and writhing in pain. There were four or five shots. I must have been in the house, looking out the window. I can still picture it, though. I don't think my parents were home at the time, but they found out. That was kind of a turning point that led to putting the house on the market. I think the safety of their children is what it came

99

down to."

That summer had a high point, unrelated to my eighth-grade class—my eldest sister's wedding. This was the dream of every girl at our school, to be the bride in a wedding in our beautiful church. My friends weren't invited to the reception, a dinner at a local restaurant, but they were all welcome at the church and wouldn't have missed it. I was the first one to have a sister get married. The ceremony was on a Saturday afternoon in August and the church was not air-conditioned. Chicago is not a terribly hot place, but that day the church was stifling. I really thought I might faint during the ceremony. Luckily, I did not, and neither did the bride. She wore a white lace "a-line" dress, the skirt just above the knees, with a short but wide veil, and her bridesmaids, including my other sister, wore similar dresses in powder blue with sun hats. The groom and his attendants wore powder blue tuxes. It was all very 1960s.

August of 1968 also brought an event that Chicago has become infamous for—the '68 Democratic National Convention. There were more riots, this time featuring the city's policemen and college kids protesting the war. Conventions are held in different cities every four years; it was just Chicago's luck that they landed this one, but the city is forever linked to this historic and violent event. Well, the violence probably had something to do with the heavy-handed reaction by the Chicago police department and Mayor Daley, but who knows how another city's leaders might have handled the protestors. Our neighborhood was pretty removed from downtown, where the protests and riots were happening, but we were able to watch on television, like the rest of the country, and knew it was not far away.

More important to my friends and me, that August was when Laura moved away. Her brother getting jumped on their block was the turning point for her parents. She knew all that time, more than two years, they would be moving. She was glad they waited to let her finish eighth grade with us. Still, she was the first of our group to leave and was not part of our freshman year in high school. The big question for her parents was where to go. Many of the families in our parish would end up in Beverly, a safer neighborhood with nicer houses that was not far from ours and still in the city. Laura hoped her parents would choose to move there, but they moved to a southern suburb instead. It was closer to where her father worked, and her mother felt it was more affordable. Her older brothers were going to Catholic high schools, which was expensive and, if they moved to Beverly, they'd have to pay for her to go to Catholic school, too. They didn't consider the high schools in the city safe. Her parents were nice about it, but they said, "There is this wonderful new high school and the bus will pick you up and take you, so why don't you just go there?" Laura felt really lost after moving, she missed her friends. She lived too far to come back to see us; it wasn't safe to go alone on the train, and none of us drove yet. Now our world was definitely different; we were losing touch with our closest friends.

Chapter 5

HIGH SCHOOL

Laura was the only one of my group of close friends who moved before high school started. Our graduating class (seventy percent white, thirty percent black) got along well and the danger we were feeling in the neighborhood didn't seem too bad. We were still allowed to walk most places with our friends that summer. I don't know what our parents were thinking, but we kids were hoping the people who moved away were wrong. The neighborhood would not get more dangerous just because blacks had moved in. It would be integrated, but we would be safe living there, at least through high school, which is what mattered most to us. We held on to that hope for a few more months.

In the fall, we went off to high school, ready to conquer the world, like most fourteen-year-olds. In the parochial system in Chicago, high school began in ninth grade, and families chose where to send their children, with input from us, or so we thought. There wasn't one Catholic school that was an obvious choice for our neighborhood, as our grammar school had been. There were only a few that were within a reasonable distance, though. There may have been a difference in cost, also, but I was oblivious to that. Wherever we went, we would have to ride a bus. Parents in those days did not consider it their responsibility to drive their kids to school. If you had six or eight or more children, the logistics were impossible, and the moms had too much to do, anyway. Imagine the laundry. My school had a private bus that picked us up, but some kids had to ride the city bus, and the boys sometimes hitchhiked down Stony Island to their school.

As girls, our choices were primarily between the two closest all-girls high schools or the only Catholic co-ed school on the South Side. Public schools were not even considered. It was not that our parents were ultra-religious; it was just part of the culture. Most of them had also gone to Catholic schools, which they considered better and, now, safer. My two older sisters had both chosen the same girls' high school. I don't know how they made their decision, but I didn't think too hard before following them there. The girls who chose the other all-girls school had a reputation, in my humble opinion, of being partiers, not as wholesome as the girls in our school. I have absolutely no evidence to support this feeling, and don't know that I had any then, but it was enough to solidify my choice. Eileen would join me there; she had older sisters who chose it, too. Sheila chose the other girls' school, where her sisters attended, while Beth went to the co-ed school. This separation meant we would start making some new friends, but we didn't lose touch with our group from St. Felicitas. Our relationships would change, but that didn't seem to affect how close we felt. We often ran into each other after school at the Little Del, and we would be on the phone by mid-week, making plans for Friday night.

Friday nights meant Carmel socials. Carmel was one of the two all-boys schools most of our male classmates attended. The priests there apparently thought it was a good idea to host a dance every Friday where boys and girls could be together, with supervision. The school was not far away but was in a dangerous neighborhood. The Blackstone Rangers street gang was based right across the street. My dad was usually elected to drive us. It was a good thing that seat belts were not required then—we packed a lot of girls into his car every Friday evening. My dad and I picked the girls up at their houses and dropped them off afterwards; no one felt it was safe to walk around our neighborhood after dark.

Despite being obsessed with those Carmel socials, which is some indication of my priorities at that age, I was developing confidence and becoming a leader at my high school. I was president of my home room, which required giving a campaign speech and getting votes. It also meant I served on the student council with girls from the other home rooms of all of the classes, even seniors. Both Katie and Lisa, two black classmates from St. Felicitas, were on the student council with me. We Felicitas girls had made a good showing at our new domain. I would have loved to have finished high school there. Katie went on to become president of our senior class. But things in the neighborhood were not stabilizing; they were getting worse.

Moving Stories

Beth had to take a city bus to get to her high school. She tried to ride with a friend or her sister, for fun and for safety, but it didn't always work out. Once, when Beth was on the bus from school without any of her friends, a lot of black kids from the nearby public high school were getting on the bus without paying. This continued for awhile until the bus driver, apparently tired of people getting on the bus for free and thinking they were getting away with it, made everybody get off and start over paying their fares. Beth was the only white passenger on the bus, and she was scared. The bus driver was white. She pleaded with him not to make her get off the bus. She was in her Catholic school uniform and thought maybe he would feel sorry for her, but he made her get off. Although she can clearly recall how scared she was, she does not remember what happened next or how she got home that day.

One day during freshman year, while Sheila was walking to Beth's house, she was attacked from behind by a black teenage boy. She was able to get away and ran to the nearest house she knew, which was Eileen's. She pounded on the door, but no one answered. When she went back to the sidewalk, the same boy grabbed her again. He let her go when she screamed. She ran all the way to Beth's house, another two blocks, across busy Stony Island. Beth's mom called the police, who came and took Sheila on a drive around the neighborhood. She was able to describe what the boy was wearing, and he was caught. He lived right near our church, but he was not a parishioner. The Chicago Tribune ran a story about the incident, although they did not identify either Sheila or her attacker, who were both minors. The story said that her screams "probably saved her from being molested." They identified the "assailant" as "a fifteen-year-old Negro boy." As Sheila remembers it, when he was arrested, he had a gun, but the article makes no mention of any weapons. Beth remembers going with Sheila to the juvenile detention center to identify the boy.[10]

That same year, Eileen's older brother got beaten up while delivering newspapers, not far from their house. Eileen remembers that he came home so mad he got a bat and was going to go out looking for the black guys that jumped him. Her dad almost had to restrain him. That was a turning point for her parents in their attitude about the neighborhood, but it was not until Eileen was threatened that they made the decision to move. Eileen rode the private school bus with me. It was a chartered bus, so we felt very safe while we were on it. I was able to get off a block from my house, but Eileen had to ride it farther to get close to her house. One day when she was walking home after the bus dropped her off, a black boy she recognized (he lived near her) threw a bottle and it hit her. As she recalls, "Now, my dad's little baby girl getting hurt—that was too much." She was the only girl in the family, and the youngest child, what we called "the baby of the family." It took a year, but they would eventually move to Beverly, near many other white families from St. Felicitas. Like my family, hers had improved their home in our parish. Her father built an addition to it himself, over several years. They really hated to leave it. They only got to use the addition for a couple of years before the area around her house became too unsafe to stay. She feels it was really hard on her dad. But it had been obvious for a long time that they had to go—to keep their children safe.

Beth was disappointed that she didn't get to go to the girls' high school her mother and older sister had attended. She always thought she would go there, but her mother knew they would be moving soon, in the opposite direction, and it would just be too hard to get there. Beth didn't feel traumatized by the move, because, after eighth grade, her friends were all moving away, and things had changed in the neighborhood. It was actually a relief to Beth when they finally moved, things had gotten so bad. Her brothers would wait for her and her sister to get off the bus from high school, because nobody wanted to walk from where the bus stopped to the house. It wasn't safe.

Beth's mother didn't drive, so she didn't want to move to the suburbs. One great thing about Chicago is its excellent public transportation system. Beth and her many siblings used it to get places that other kids' moms drove them to. Beth's family chose a neighborhood only four miles south and west of ours, but still in the city, with stores you could walk to and easy access to buses and trains. It was considered a safe neighborhood, certainly safer than ours was by then. Beth could still take the bus to her high school, but now none of her friends rode with her. When Beth turned sixteen, about four months after the move, she got a job in a department store just a couple blocks from their new home. She worked in the stockroom on the third floor and often took the stairs. She shared this story from that time:

> "Sure enough, I go into a stairwell—to this day I won't go into a stairwell—and a black man followed me in and grabbed me. He was grabbing my legs and I started kicking him. I remember clearly that I opened my mouth to scream and absolutely nothing came out. I was kicking him, and I scrambled up the stairs and I went busting through the door on the next landing and a really nice older woman was up there and she took care of me. I knew he was after me, but you know, at that age, I really didn't know what might happen. Then I remember going home and the police were called.
>
> "When I got home, I was mostly terrified to tell my dad I lost my job. I knew I could never go back there, so I'd have to give up the job. My mom and dad were sitting there, and they didn't know how to act. The store manager had called my parents, so they knew what had happened. They

were trying to ask me 'Did he rape you?' but I didn't even know what they were trying to say. I didn't get it then, but I get it now, and I really feel for my poor mom and dad."

For Beth's parents, this meant they would need to make another move, and her mom had to somehow find the time to learn to drive, to increase their options beyond the city bus system. Five years later, they moved to a suburb about thirty minutes south of the city. By then, Beth was off at college, but there were still several children at home who had to be uprooted from their schools once again. Their original choice of a neighborhood so close to ours may seem foolish now, but individual neighborhoods in Chicago are quite distinct and a few blocks often made the difference between safety and danger. Her parents probably did not believe that white flight would continue until no whites remained anywhere on the South Side, but that is pretty close to what ultimately happened and, as it had in our neighborhood, the transition period in their new neighborhood included fear and danger for those who were caught in the middle of the change.

One day after they moved, Beth's brother Bill rode his bike back to our parish to visit some friends. On his way home he was taunted by groups of black youths at least twice but, being on a bike while they were on foot, he got away easily. He wanted to stop at the Malone's house, right next to Avalon Park, where that year's St. Felicitas eighth grade was having one of their graduation parties. As he got close, he saw a group of black teens gathered across the street from the house where the party was going on. There was a quasi-brownout of the street lights that day, so it was fairly dark with poor visibility, but Bill could see that the black kids were throwing something at the windows of the house – rocks or bottles, or both. Some Felicitas boys left the party to give chase to the rock throwers. Bill suddenly heard voices nearby; some boys from the rock-throwing group were now very close to him. He started to run while jumping on his bike to escape but lost his balance and dropped the bike. A black youth chasing him also fell, so Bill was able to get away on foot to the nearby home of a friend. When he went back later for the bike, it had been badly damaged. Angered, he carried it back to the friend's house, where he picked up some empty pop bottles and headed back to the site of the attacked party. There he joined the white St. Felicitas boys from the party, all of them now walking toward the group of black youths, throwing bottles at them and yelling expletives.

These kinds of incidents were getting to be all too common, so we all knew moving was inevitable, although we hated the idea. Sheila remembers that there were groups of adults in the parish that were still saying we should stay, and other groups who felt they had to go, white adults, including our parents. Her father was active in the Marynook Homeowners Association and had taken the position that people should not move. She didn't know they were actually going to move until about six weeks before. Her dad didn't say anything about why he had changed his mind, after advocating for staying. He didn't discuss it with his children.

In a letter she wrote to a friend that year, Sheila shared how she felt about moving and changing high schools:

> "The only thing I'm worried about is making friends. I don't know what to do. I have no idea what I'm gonna do, or who I'm gonna hang around with. When we move I'll probably just stay in on weekends. It will be such a bore! I know there's not much to do around here, but at least I hang around with some kids.
>
> "Should I have a party at my new house? If I do, I wouldn't know when to have it. Kids from Chicago wouldn't come all the way out there, because it's too far to be driven out and then picked up a couple hours later. I don't know. I'm just mixed up."

Eileen's family stayed in the parish until the end of her sophomore year. She started that year at the same high school she attended as a freshman, but there was an incident on the bus to school, so her mother insisted that she change to a school closer to their new home. Her dad resisted moving for a long time He wasn't there enough to see what was going on; he worked a lot of hours and sometimes on the weekends. Her mom was the one who would be there when the kids would come home crying that someone stole their bike, or somebody hit them. Right before they moved, Eileen's older sister was assaulted at knifepoint. Now her mom felt they had waited too long. It happened right on 83rd street, at the train station. Her mom had felt trapped and had been pleading with her dad, who she felt had his head in the sand. She just finally gave him an ultimatum, she was going out to look at houses; they were moving. Eileen didn't want it to happen. She had a core group of friends who still lived in the neighborhood, hoping to hang on. They just really didn't want to leave, they wanted to cling to memories and kept thinking, "It's not that bad, let's not give up on it." But her mother had seen one too many incidents involving her children.

Eileen remembers that groups of black teenagers sometimes roamed through the neighborhood with baseball bats and chains. We didn't know them, they came from outside the parish, or on the edges of it, just swaggering, walking around the neighborhood and scaring people. They were kids, but they were big, it was intimidating. Eileen recalls that the atmosphere changed from "Hey, we want to be friends, we want to be part of the community" to "There are more of us now, so we are going to start intimidating the hell out of all of you and make you want to leave." And it had that effect, after a while.

Another friend who lived near Sheila stayed in the parish until the end of her junior year. She was the last of our group of friends to leave the parish. She recalls holding out hope that things would get better, that all of the unrest was just a phase, since it was such a nice neighborhood:

> "My family stayed longer than any of my friends' families. It was only a year, but it made a big difference, because I was in a cocoon then. I can

109

remember my dad telling me not to even go out into the yard. The neighbors were all black, with young boys. I took the bus to school only one time. Everyone on the bus was black except one white girl, also coming from my school. A black girl stood up and said, 'Say it loud, I'm black and I'm proud.' Then the other white girl on the bus stood up and said, 'Say it louder, I'm white and I'm prouder.' Nobody reacted."

Her parents put a sign up on their house that said: "This is our home," underlined home, "it is not for sale," because people kept coming to the door trying to convince them to sell. Several white families had signs like that. The activity of the blockbusters had really picked up. They were going door to door telling people they had to get out before they lost even more money on their houses. The blockbusters and other speculators were, of course, buying the houses at deflated prices and selling them at higher prices to the middle-class blacks who had few other choices.

My friend recalls several instances of bricks being thrown right through the front windows of houses that had those signs. Rumor was that it was being done by blacks, but I wonder now if it might have been the blockbusters, or someone they hired to do it. These attacks were just too personal; they felt targeted, and her parents decided they would have to move. They were extremely sad to leave the St. Felicitas parish; her father and his family had lived there since the 1940s.

Oklahoma Bound

My sisters reminded me of a day when two groups of black teenagers came through the neighborhood with baseball bats and chains and ended up meeting at the corner right in front of our house. We were watching out of the window, in shock. My dad was at work, and my mother had left my oldest sister in charge for a short time, a rare occurrence. She was, of course, very upset that something so possibly dangerous happened while she was away. The police came, and the teenagers dispersed before anything violent occurred. This may have been the same event of kids with bats and chains that Eileen recalled, she lived near us, or this may have happened more than once. I believe now that some of these events were staged by the real estate speculators who wanted us to move.[11] They were trying to scare us, and it worked. But I do not believe the speculators were responsible for all of the events that scared us. There were too many and they were too personal. I don't know if this event or the riots after Reverend King's assassination, or any other specific event sped up my parents' decision to move. They never seemed afraid to me. But they had been talking about moving to Oklahoma "someday" before any of this had started. I guess it was starting to feel like a good time to go.

I continued to work in my dad's grocery store up until the day we moved. That last summer, after freshman year, also meant lots of trips to Rainbow Beach with my friends. We were still a close-knit group. One of our friends moved to a house just a block from our favorite part of the beach, so we saw a lot of her. We met boys at the beach; some of them were the same boys we had met at the Carmel socials. They were from Catholic high schools, but had not gone to grammar school with us, so somehow seemed more grown up, more sophisticated. I "dated" one of them who also lived close to the beach. We didn't really date; our parents didn't allow us to go out with boys at night, but we saw each other at the beach and found ways to occasionally be alone. I remember one time we were actually at the beach at night. There must have been a special event going on, as this was not the norm. We usually rode the bus to the beach, but it wasn't safe to ride it at night, so my mom came to pick us up. When she got there, I was nowhere to be seen, having snuck off into the dark area of the park adjacent to the beach with my boyfriend. He actually heard my friends calling me, and I rushed back to where they were. I don't recall ever seeing my mother so mad at me. She had good reason, although I felt perfectly safe at the time. At fifteen, I didn't realize my own vulnerability. She apparently got over it, since later that summer I was allowed to

111

go with this same boy and his older sister and her boyfriend to my first live concert—Jim Morrison and the Doors at the Auditorium Theater. I didn't know much about the Doors then; my parents obviously had no idea who they were.

Life was still good, and we continued to be normal teenagers, despite the cloud of "moving" over everyone's head. There hadn't been any assassinations in over a year and the war news was starting to look better; we weren't winning but maybe we could stop losing so many lives. Doesn't really sound too positive, but the bar was pretty low after 1968. The space race was back on, too, and we were definitely winning that. I have a great memory of Neil Armstrong's first steps on the moon. My dad's grocery store had a bowling team and they let me play, despite the fact that I was never any good. I loved going to the bowling alley and being a part of what felt like a very grown-up activity. We were at the bowling alley watching a grainy black-and-white television in the snack bar when Armstrong made his historic statement: "One small step for man, one giant leap for mankind." It was just before 10 PM, Chicago time, July 20, 1969—about a week before my dad and I were to leave Chicago for good.

I always knew we would move to Oklahoma, so I don't think I even considered that there might be another option for me. My parents met near the end of World War II, while my dad was in the Army, stationed near where my mom grew up. There weren't any eligible men left in Mom's hometown of Atoka, although the lucky ones would make it home safely within the next few years. My mother's pre-war boyfriend did not make it back. My father's pre-war girlfriend sent him a "Dear John" letter while he was still overseas. It was a rough time for romance. So, Mom and her friends would hang out at the downtown Atoka bus station on Saturday night to see who might be coming into town. I guess there was not much else to do in a small town like that. One night in 1945, my dad and his army buddies got off the bus in Atoka. My parents were married a few months later.

My mother told me her family thought my dad was probably mafia, being from Chicago. Although he was mostly German (and/or Polish) with hazel eyes, he had dark curly hair, which I'm sure looked "eye-talian" to them. I imagine they were not pleased that she became Catholic to marry him, either. But that all happened long before I was born. My dad claimed he had been willing to stay in Oklahoma for my mom, but he didn't have any connections there to help him get started in business; my grandfather worked on the railroad and didn't know anyone connected to money. Dad could have gone to college on the new G.I. Bill, but he had just lost over four years to the army; he was ready to get his life started. College would have to be his dream for his children. So, my parents went to Chicago, where my dad had grown up and where he had worked, before the war, for a grocer in his old neighborhood. Mr. Reuther knew a good worker when he saw one. He was not only a willing mentor, he loaned Dad money to start his own grocery store. In 1946, Bill's Food & Liquor was born not far from Rainbow Beach on East 79th—where it would grow into a supermarket and support our family very well—until we had to move away. By the time we moved, that neighborhood was becoming just as dangerous as the one where we lived.

Later that summer, when we were in our new home on the outskirts of Oklahoma City, the news would be filled with the gruesome murders by Charles Manson and his cult, followed closely by the free-love and drug-infused Woodstock Music Festival. But, for me, moving was all that would matter. I spent the rest of summer vacation pulling weeds in our new backyard where my parents were trying to establish a lawn in the Oklahoma red clay. I remember thinking that the sky was much bluer in Oklahoma than in Chicago, but it was also hotter, and that red clay was hard. Digging up weeds there was not an idle pastime. It certainly wasn't like a day at Rainbow Beach.

Our neighborhood was brand new, so there were other teenagers new to the area that I met and hung out with some, but it was not the same as being with my St. Felicitas friends. My mother gave me an important piece of advice that year. She told me that I would never have friends quite like the ones I grew up with, and I should not lose them. I took that to heart and kept in touch with letters and Christmas cards over the years. After college, when I finally had the resources to travel, I starting going back to visit. Although only a few of my friends live near one another, we try to get the whole group together when I am there. It always seems we can just pick up where we left off. Now we try to do that every year, as we know these friendships are indeed precious and the years will someday end. I didn't often agree with my mother, but she was certainly right this time. These are friends I will always cherish and I'm glad I heeded her advice and did not take them for granted.

When we are together, despite the fifty years of life that have intervened, we end up talking with nostalgia about our days at St. Felicitas. Although our memories are mostly of our idyllic childhood, they will always be clouded by the danger we faced together and the loss we felt as each one of us moved away from our beloved childhood parish.

THE END

Afterword

EXPERIENCES OF OUR
AFRICAN-AMERICAN CLASSMATES

Two of my African-American St. Felicitas classmates agreed to
read a draft of this book, to provide me feedback and share some
memories of their own. Although two people obviously cannot
speak for all 22 of our African-American classmates, their
experiences add depth and counterpoint to my memories and those
of my white friends. I have given them pseudonyms, like the rest of
the children in this book.

Diana

Diana was shocked to hear about our experiences of
violence in the neighborhood. Her parents didn't allow her to walk
around the streets like we did; she went home after school, where
she played with friends and her sisters or did homework. On the
weekends, by the time she was a preteen, she and her sisters babysat
for neighbors. They didn't go to dances or parties. I assume that her
parents were well aware of what was happening around them, being
one of the first black families in the parish. They appear to have
been keeping their children away from the turmoil occurring around
us all and protecting them as best they could from the hatred that
Chicagoans in general had demonstrated to blacks. We white girls
considered Diana a friend, but, once we got into seventh grade, she
was not part of our clique. She would have been welcome at our
parties, though I don't remember seeing her at any.

Diana did remember some negative things about that time.
Someone threw a rock through one of her family's windows shortly
after they moved into the neighborhood (in 1963). She believes it

was a white student at St. Felicitas, someone who knew one of her older siblings. A more personal memory had to do with the birthday party of one of her white classmates. All of the white girls in her class were invited. Diana, the sole African-American student in the class, was the only one not invited. It made her feel embarrassed at the time, and she still feels the hurt of this affront. Despite these bad memories, she did not grow up fearful of her environment.

When I asked her about cheerleading, she said it would never have occurred to her or her sisters that they could be St. Felicitas cheerleaders. They weren't particularly disappointed by this; they just took it as a fact. Her experience of her time at St. Felicitas School includes fond memories of the church, the nuns, the bakery, the playground—much like mine—but does not include a close-knit group of friends or the strong feelings of attachment to the parish that my white friends and I had. She was excited to leave St. Felicitas behind and join her sisters at a high school a little farther away from the parish than the high schools the rest of us girls chose. Later, she attended college out of state, at the insistence of her parents. No one in her family lives in or near Chicago now.

Steven

My classmate Steven had a radically different experience from that of Diana. He was very involved in parish activities, as an altar boy and athlete, which meant he was often walking between his home, not far from one of the public grammar schools, and our school grounds or Avalon Park. He was not immune to the violence we experienced; in fact, he experienced a double dose of violence. White kids (from the public schools) harassed him for being a black kid in the neighborhood, and the same black kids who were picking on us white kids wanted to beat him up for going to a white school and being friends with the Groundsmen. He wasn't a Groundsman, of course, and he knew that he couldn't be, the same way Diana knew she couldn't be a cheerleader. He accepted that, even as he understood it to be unjust. His experience of this "double jeopardy" was at its worst the day that the Reverend Dr. Martin Luther King,

116

Jr. was assassinated—Steven was pursued by both black and white kids on his way home from school.

Steven remembers some of the white boys at St. Felicitas, who he considered his friends, using racial invectives. They weren't being used against him but were said in his presence—something he found difficult to understand, especially within the context of a Catholic school. According to Steven, the African Americans in our parish considered the Groundsmen a gang. They did not believe its members were involved in criminal activities, but all of the members were white, and they protected their territory. Some of the older Groundsmen were known to have hateful feelings toward African Americans, even those in our school. Steven had interactions with one of them, who made it clear he hated blacks. Luckily, there were also Groundsmen willing to intervene:

> "I remember that it was the O'Brien family, the boys that were near my age, who protected me from this guy, and I made a point of not being around the Grounds outside of school hours, unless some member of the O'Brien family was there."

Steven reflected on the actions of the black kids against white kids in the neighborhood by wondering if they felt justified in their dislike of us (without even knowing us) based on what they had seen (or heard about) white people doing to black people without knowing them. As a specific example, the bullying behavior of black kids refusing to yield space on the sidewalk, forcing us to walk in the grass or in the street, as reminiscent of a common practice of whites against blacks in some all-white neighborhoods and other public places where whites were dominant.

Steven's memories refute my contention that the white kids within our school were always welcoming to our black classmates. Despite some painful memories of this troubling time, Steven says that he cherishes his memories of St. Felicitas and his classmates.

Concluding Thoughts

Diana shared with me that she found the stories of violence in this book difficult to read. If her children had been subjected to anything remotely akin to what we experienced, she said she would have moved them away from the situation much sooner than our parents did. Steven also felt the stories shared here make it clear why our parents made the difficult decision to move—for the safety of their children.

Heppner Family, May 1955, Connie's First Communion

Our house at 82nd & Dorchester, Winter of 1961–2

My Kindergarten
Pinafore

My First
Communion Dress

St. Felicitas Church, school in background, taken in 2004

St. Felicitas School,
taken in 1992

The Little Del,
taken in 1969

My Eighth-Grade Photo,
wearing the dress I made for
the basketball banquet

My Seventh-Grade
Class

"The Big Game,"
March 17, 1968

Photo Courtesy of
The McGuire
Family Archives

PART TWO

MY RESEARCH

CHAPTER 6

GEOGRAPHY & REAL ESTATE

The Great Migration

After Reconstruction, Jim Crow laws became the norm in the South, severely restricting rights for blacks. There was little, if any, economic opportunity, and the Klu Klux Klan ensured that any perceived transgression of law or social norm was dealt with harshly. It is not at all surprising that blacks began moving to cities in the North, Midwest and West whenever they were able. This was not a decision made lightly; in addition to leaving behind family and community, black southerners were abandoning dreams of landownership.[12] In total, it is estimated that six million blacks moved out of the South during what is now known as the Great Migration, approximately 1870 to 1970.[13]

The Great Migration sped up when World War I created a demand for workers in the industrial cities. "The Chicago Defender" delivered its papers in the South, advertising job opportunities to blacks, and Chicago's black population doubled from 50,000 at the start of WWI to 100,000 by the war's end. Although there actually were job opportunities for blacks when they arrived, Chicago was not a welcoming place. Housing conditions were bad for the entire working class. Things were even worse for blacks, whose housing choices were legally restricted to a small section of the city just south of downtown, known as the Black Belt. That area became severely overcrowded, and many absentee landlords allowed their properties to decay, resulting in ghetto conditions.[14]

Migration of blacks out of the South increased again after World War II, due to wartime technological advances that caused a loss of jobs in farming. Between 1940 and 1960, the number of blacks in Chicago nearly tripled—from 278,000 to over 800,000. When this wave began, blacks still lived mostly in the segregated Black Belt.[15]

In 1958, the first black residents moved into the South Shore neighborhood, about two miles from the home my parents bought in St. Felicitas a few years earlier. South Shore was just south of Woodlawn, which by then was predominantly black. The residents of South Shore believed blacks would move gradually south and east through their neighborhood and viewed the process as unstoppable. Some "likened it . . . to the growth of a cancer;" a rabbi in the neighborhood described it as a "spreading ink blot."[16]

Restrictive Covenants

Crowded conditions citywide, compounded by the returning WWI veterans, led to a building boom in Chicago in the twenties and thirties. In my neighborhood and others on the South Side, this era saw the building of classic Chicago bungalows like the one where I grew up. St. Felicitas Parish was founded in 1919; its grammar school opened in 1924. The surrounding neighborhood, Avalon Park, was swampland and a city dump until the early teens.[17]

About this time, the U.S. Supreme Court ruled that residential segregation ordinances, like the one that kept Chicago's blacks in the Black Belt, were unconstitutional. Not to be deterred, real estate professionals in Chicago began promoting restrictive racial covenants. These covenants, which were written into property deeds, prohibited the property's sale or lease to blacks.[8] At this time, the Black Belt extended to 47th Street, where it was closing in on the University of Chicago. The University contributed to the homeowners associations of nearby white neighborhoods that were supporting the use of restrictive covenants, causing some to refer to the covenants as "The University of Chicago's agreements to get rid of Negros."[5]

By the 1940s, Chicago led the nation in the use of restrictive covenants; nearly half of all neighborhoods prohibited black residents.[18] Finally, in 1948, the covenants were ruled unconstitutional by the U.S. Supreme Court.[8] Woodlawn, the neighborhood just south of the University, integrated rapidly after that. By 1960, it was 89% black.[19]

Redlining & Contract Sales

As part of Roosevelt's New Deal in the 1930s, billions of dollars of assistance were provided to banks and homeowners—both struggling to recover from the Great Depression. This legislation created the Home Owners' Loan Corporation (HOLC) to standardize mortgage lending practices, with the goal of preventing another economic collapse. Real estate appraisals were now required before loans could be made and, to assist the appraisers, the HOLC developed maps of 200 cities that rated neighborhoods based on perceived stability. Known as Security Maps, they gave each distinct neighborhood a letter and color code: A, or, green was considered best; homes in B, or blue-coded neighborhoods, were "still desirable"; C, or yellow, meant "definitely declining"; and D, or red, meant "hazardous."[20] The use of these codes came to be known as "redlining."

HOLC used these maps to refinance a million homes, making a profit for the government and helping to stabilize the housing market. It was an understandably popular government program.[20] HOLC lasted only a few years, but the Federal Housing Administration (FHA) continued to use their maps. The FHA had also been created at this time to protect banks by insuring loans and to help first-time homeowners by allowing for lower down payments and lower interest rates than traditional loans.[18]

Although this sounds quite positive, and HOLC was considered a successful government program, there was racial bias written into redlining. Neighborhoods where blacks lived, or that were "threatened by Negro encroachment" were rated D, redlined, regardless of the number or income level of the black families living there. Those areas were considered risky or likely to decline in value. Loans were rarely made in redlined neighborhoods— either to buy homes or for home improvements.[21] Eventually, redlining went beyond FHA-backed loans and spread to the entire mortgage industry. It was nearly impossible for young families to buy in redlined areas. If mortgage loans were available there at all, they were for only 15 or 20 year terms and required 40–50% of the home's value as a down payment.[20]

HOLC was taking the notions of racial and ethnic "worth" then generally accepted and applying them to real estate value. The result was that black Americans were barred from the opportunities to buy homes that were being afforded to whites in more favorable areas.[20,21] The fear that whites had of the value of their homes declining if blacks moved in was, at this time, not just a racist rant—government policies made sure of it.[18]

When the HOLC maps were drawn up in the early forties, my neighborhood, Avalon Park, appeared on them as rated B, or blue. The closest A-rated neighborhood to us was Beverly, on the western edge of the city; the growing south suburbs were also rated A. Apparently, the only places rated A by HOLC were those with new homes and homes still being built. There were already many redlined areas around St. Felicitas when the maps were drawn.[20]

During this era, roughly the forties and fifties, blacks were essentially locked out of the mortgage market—and many whites had difficulty selling their homes, because the blacks who were the likely buyers could not get loans. This created an opportunity for real estate speculators. The speculators would buy homes from whites, who either needed to move or just wanted to get out with some value left in their properties. The whites were paid depressed prices, because they had no other options. The homes could then be sold directly to blacks, who had even fewer options, for a profit. The profit, of course, went to the speculator, not the previous property owner.[21]

Since they could not get mortgages, blacks bought through what were known as contract sales. These sales were really more like "rent to own," since the seller held the deed until the house was completely paid off. If a payment was missed, either for the note itself or for assessed repairs, taxes or insurance, the house could be taken away from the contract buyer, with no return of equity. When a home was repossessed in this way, it could be sold again— resulting in even more profits for real estate speculators. Blacks buying on contract had all of the responsibility of home ownership without the rights. It's been estimated that as many as 85% of black home buyers in Chicago bought their houses under contract sales before they were outlawed in 1962.[18, 21]

Fair Housing & Open Occupancy

The rental market was not exempt from the racist policies of the early twentieth century. As Chicago's black population moved southward from the Black Belt, they were paying inflated prices on both home purchases and apartment rentals. This "color tax" was due in part to the demand for housing by upwardly mobile blacks exceeding the supply.[16] The supply, of course, was limited by restrictive covenants at first, then by redlining, both of which impacted homebuyers as well as landlords wishing to buy or improve rental properties.

To combat this, Chicago passed a fair housing ordinance in 1963.The law had many detractors. The Chicago Real Estate Board led the opposition, saying it was a restriction of human rights. The president of one neighborhood association alleged that the ordinance was being proposed by communists who wanted to destroy individual rights. Despite the passage of the new ordinance, landlords continued to discriminate, only renting to blacks when they could no longer find white renters. The ordinance also prohibited blockbusting, but it gave the Chicago Commission on Human Relations the responsibility of enforcement, and they were known to go easy on those accused, merely accepting the blockbuster's word that he would not do it again.[8, 16]

In the mid-sixties, a sociologist surveyed the "real estate men" working on the South Side. They perceived two distinctly separate housing markets—one for blacks, one for whites. This "dual market" was supported by real estate textbooks at that time and had even been endorsed by the National Association of Real Estate Boards. Very few of the survey respondents even mentioned the Chicago fair housing ordinance. The researcher concluded that the ordinance meant little to them, and they were not concerned with complying with it.[16]

Given the ineffectiveness of Chicago's fair housing ordinance, a fight began for an open occupancy law in Illinois, to prohibit any discrimination in housing. It was during this time that The Reverend Dr. Martin Luther King, Jr. began the Chicago Freedom Movement to fight the unscrupulous real estate practices and threats of violence that were confining blacks to ghettos. The movement and its marches brought the housing discrimination in northern cities to light for the nation. King and the Southern Christian Leadership Conference felt that, if they could get Chicago to change, the rest of the nation would follow. During a peaceful protest, Reverend King was physically attacked by whites and told reporters he had "never seen as much hatred and hostility on the part of so many people." An agreement for some changes to relieve the ghetto conditions was finally reached by the SCLC and Mayor Daley, but it was not in writing and legally unenforceable. Daley was said to have cheered Reverend King's failure in his city.[2, 3, 23]

Before supporters could get an open occupancy law passed in Illinois, the 1968 Fair Housing Act was passed by the federal government, making such state laws unnecessary. This federal legislation was signed by President Johnson, shortly after the assassination of Reverend King and the riots that followed. The Fair Housing Act, along with a Supreme Court case (Jones v Mayer) made housing discrimination illegal countrywide.[8]

Deteriorating Neighborhoods

There seems to have been a general belief among whites in Chicago that, when blacks moved in, neighborhoods became full of rundown and boarded-up buildings and were, on the whole, "blighted." They based this, of course, on the black neighborhoods they drove through on the near South Side and West Side of the city. The reason this was so was perhaps too complex for them determine at the time but seems obvious in hindsight. The combined impact of restricted covenants and redlining had forced black families to cram themselves into older homes that were subdivided to make room for those who continued to stream into the city from the South. Other immigrant groups had lived in similar conditions in the past, but they could legally move out of the ghettos once they saved and earned enough to afford better housing. Blacks were not so lucky.

In the survey of realtors mentioned above, the realtors said the higher rents paid by blacks were due to increased maintenance costs. The cost increase, they said, was the result of an increased number of children, vandalism and a lack of respect for property. In conversations with the realtors, however, the researcher who conducted the survey was told that it was standard practice to decrease building services when blacks moved in, and that some white janitors would not maintain a black-occupied building at the same levels they had for whites, due to their own racial prejudices.[16]

This lack of maintenance, when combined with overcrowding and the lack of access to loans available to improve properties, led to deterioration of rental housing. To keep up with contract payments, black homeowners worked multiple jobs, took in boarders and deferred maintenance on their homes; all of this contributed to deterioration of private homes. With both rentals and owner-occupied homes in decline, entire neighborhoods started to deteriorate.[21]

Urban renewal projects were seen by politicians as a solution to blighted neighborhoods, but they often destroyed the limited available affordable housing in the process. The majority black neighborhood Woodlawn had already begun to deteriorate. All of these factors led Chicago's black citizens to continue to seek housing in neighborhoods further south.

Public Schools

Better public schools were also part of the reason blacks were so anxious to move into white neighborhoods. Benjamin C. Willis, superintendent of Chicago's schools from the mid-fifties until the mid-sixties, was known to favor segregation. Chicago had long had a policy of neighborhood schools which created de facto school segregation, since most neighborhoods were segregated. When planning new schools in the Black Belt, the district failed to consider the crowded conditions and multiple families living in the available housing. Willis resisted redrawing school boundaries or busing children to less crowded schools.[8]

Schools in black neighborhoods became overcrowded, and black children were often forced to attend school on what were known as split shifts, attending only part of the day so that other children could use the same facilities at a different time. This, of course, led both to poorer education and unsupervised children, since most black families needed two working adults to survive. As Chicago's neighborhoods changed quickly from predominantly white to predominantly black, the schools re-segregated along with them. A study released in 1964 found that, despite the ten years since the Brown v Board of Education decision, schools were still segregated and the quality of education in predominantly black schools was inferior to that of predominantly white schools.[24]

Eventually, some redrawing of the school lines could not be avoided, which meant integrating white schools. The result, however, sometimes meant that white kids would have to walk past their old schools to schools that already had black students. In her memoir of this time, Linda Gartz tells of being assigned to a new school in the early sixties with a reputation for having black gang activity. Her father was distressed, saying, "They expect us to send a young white girl into that dangerous, colored neighborhood? She could be raped!" Her family decided to send her to a private school instead. This required her to travel seven miles on two buses, a 45 minute trip each way.[15]

School   redistricting   created   a   perfect   scene   for blockbusters, who wanted to scare whites into moving—white kids had to walk several blocks to new schools when their old schools were closer, and black kids walked through white neighborhoods to get to their newly assigned schools. The rumors of violence in the schools also spread fear. The tension was so high at some schools that police stood outside at dismissal to be sure black kids and white kids headed home along different paths.[15]

In the mid-sixties, white families in the Marynook section of my neighborhood petitioned the school board to allow their children to go to a different public school, which had better "balance" racially and was considered better academically than the one in their district. Middle-class black families in our neighborhood didn't want to send their children to the neighborhood public schools either. There were rumors that the public school a block from my house might have to go to split shifts.[25-27] The African-American family that lived next door to us sent their children to their grandparents in Mississippi to attend school.

Public Housing

In 1938, when the Chicago Housing Authority (CHA) began building subsidized housing, they followed the federal government's "Neighborhood Composition Rule," meaning the demographics of those allowed to live in government subsidized housing should match the racial composition of the neighborhood where it was built. Consequently, one of the CHA's first projects, Trumbull Park Homes, was originally all white. In the mid-1950s, a few brave black families moved in. The apartments there would have been better physically than their Black Belt rentals, but the neighborhood was not at all welcoming. The 1959 book, "Trumbull Park," by Frank London Brown, provides a fictionalized version of the experiences of the author and his family, who moved there in 1954. The author conveys the feeling of constant fear they lived with. The white residents of both the housing and the surrounding neighborhood continually threw homemade firebombs at the apartments of the black families, which made loud noises, reminding the black families that they were not welcome—and not safe—day or night. The harassment went on for years and the cost of the police protection required to prevent outright rioting is sometimes blamed for safety issues in other parts of the city.[28, 29]

Later, nearly all public housing in Chicago would be built in poor, black neighborhoods. This era included building the numerous drab complexes that covered multiple blocks of South State Street, including the mammoth towers of the Robert Taylor Homes, the largest public housing project in the United States.[29] It would eventually house many African-American families but, while it was being built, it displaced hundreds of poor families on the South Side, most of them black. Sociologist Arnold Hirsch calls public housing "the second ghetto"—larger than the Black Belt but just as impermeable.[18] In 1966, a lawsuit was filed against the CHA alleging that their policies had restricted opportunities for African Americans in Chicago. One of the longest running federal court cases in U.S. history, a settlement agreement was finally approved in January of 2019, giving the CHA until 2024 to "offset the impacts of racial segregation caused by its historic building and tenant practices."[30]

Resistance

Trumbull Park was, of course, not the only instance in which blacks moving into white neighborhoods were met with resistance. Here are a few of the more notorious examples:

- In 1947, a few black veterans and their families moved into a housing project in Fernwood, part of the Roseland neighborhood. Three nights of rioting followed, requiring 1,000 police officers to control.[18]
- After the Supreme Court outlawed restrictive covenants in 1949, a black family

moved into the Park Manor, a neighborhood just south of Woodlawn. Their furniture was burned on their lawn during riots that involved 2,000 whites.[3]

- Also in 1949, a few blacks were invited to a meeting at a labor organizer's home in Englewood. Rumor spread that he had sold his home to blacks. Riots erupted, with up to 10,000 whites milling outside his home for three nights.[7]

- In 1951, thousands of whites in Cicero, a suburb twenty minutes west of downtown, attacked an apartment building where a black family lived.[18]

Role of the Suburbs

While upwardly-mobile blacks were buying homes in neighborhoods like mine, some whites were being lured to the suburbs where they found better, newer houses. Marynook aside, our neighborhood was part of the "bungalow belt" built in the 1920s, and the houses, though sturdy, looked drab next to the shiny new ones in the suburbs. The South Side was also deteriorating, at least partly because of the environmental impact of the soot from the steel mills and the railroads that went right through its neighborhoods.[16]

The typical bungalow, like ours, had three bedrooms and one bathroom. The large families in our neighborhood were crowded into them. The suburbs offered larger homes for these growing families. Public schools there were considered better than those in the city. Catholic families, who would never have sent their children to the public high schools in Chicago, did so in the suburbs, saving them tuition dollars. Expressways were being built, making it possible to get into downtown and other places of employment. Businesses began moving to the suburbs too, so not everyone needed to commute into the city.[8]

All of this was expedited by those folks at the Federal Housing Administration and the HOLC surveyors who had labeled these growing suburban communities A, or green. The same policies that thwarted home ownership for blacks encouraged it for whites, who began populating these new areas in the 1950s. In the first decade after WWII, nine million Americans left cities for suburbs. This was an era of unprecedented homeownership—in 1930 only 30 percent of Americans owned their own homes; by 1960, 60 percent did.[7, 18]

Concluding Thoughts

The commonly used expression "integration is the time between when the first black family moves in and when the last white family moves out," appears to be fitting summary for this chapter. Studies have shown that the segregation of housing in American cities did not change between 1940 and 1960, it merely reversed—all-white neighborhoods became all-black neighborhoods. This has also been termed "re-segregation" and has been studied by social scientists as far back as the early 1940s.[16] Neighborhoods changed, block-by-block, in a fairly predictable pattern. Sometimes the arrival of the first black families was met with violence, but not always.

In hindsight, all of this can be seen as leading to the inevitable changes in our parish. As children, we had no idea that any of these big-picture things were going on, or that something larger than St. Felicitas parish even existed. As I've tried to convey in this book, the racial change in the neighborhood was very gradual and did not seem unusual to us kids. But then it sped up. The first year that we had African-American classmates in my grade at St. Felicitas, they were two children in our third-grade class of 107. Our eighth-grade-graduating class in 1968 would be 23 black students, 53 white. African-American residents of our neighborhood, Avalon Park, numbered only 6 in 1960; in 1970 there were approximately 12,000, representing 83 percent of the neighborhood population. By 1980 that had increased to 96 percent.[31]

SOUTH SIDE NEIGHBORHOODS

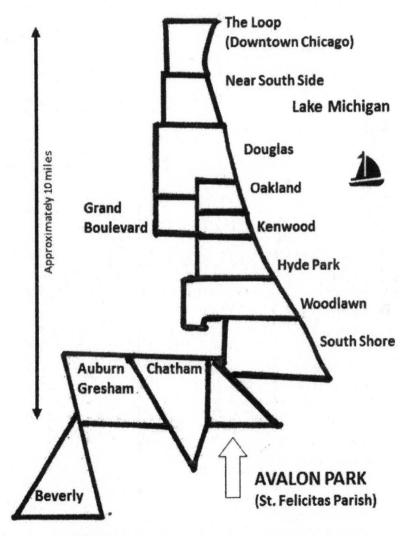

The Loop
(Downtown Chicago)

Near South Side

Lake Michigan

Douglas

Oakland

Grand
Boulevard

Kenwood

Hyde Park

Woodlawn

South Shore

Approximately 10 miles

Auburn
Gresham

Chatham

Beverly

AVALON PARK
(St. Felicitas Parish)

Map hand drawn by the author. Size and scale are
approximate. Only neighborhoods discussed in this
book are shown.

CHAPTER 7

BLOCKBUSTERS & NEIGHBORHOOD ASSOCIATIONS

Our neighborhood and others on the South Side fought back against unscrupulous real estate agents and speculators, or blockbusters, who the press labeled "panic-peddlers." They were fought through neighborhood associations and other community groups focused on "stabilizing" neighborhoods. The actions of one of these groups in my neighborhood, The Marynook Homeowners Association, were considered successful, at least in the beginning. Similar groups formed in Beverly and Oak Park, which are now integrated neighborhoods and considered desirable places to live by both blacks and whites. This made me wonder if these groups actually had good intentions, as opposed to the fictional Clybourne Park Improvement Association depicted in "A Raisin in the Sun," whose members felt blacks would be better off living in "their own" neighborhoods.[1]

The Blockbusters

Early on, the term "blockbuster" was applied to those real estate salesmen who were willing to sell a house to blacks on a city block where only white families lived. Doing so violated the Chicago Real Estate Board's code of ethics. Their policy, in place since 1917, was the same as that of the National Association of Real Estate Boards. The blockbusters were reaping tremendous profits for their work—and they were not waiting for whites to decide it was time to move; they were actively working to encourage the transition of neighborhoods from white to black. Once the first black family moved onto a block, their tactics were ramped up, and many whites, believing their messages, agreed to sell. Blocks, then neighborhoods, transitioned from all white to all black at a rapid pace.[8]

In 1959, the year I started kindergarten at St. Felicitas, the Chicago Daily News ran an entire series exposing these unethical real estate tactics and giving their perpetrators the name "panic-peddlers." The paper broke the panic-peddlers' methods into three phases: first, softening up, which was introducing the idea that the neighborhood was going to change; second, building fear to get the first white homeowner to actually sell, often directly to speculators; then third, buying up as many properties as possible on that block or in that neighborhood. The tactics of blockbusters ranged from scaring white homeowners by telling them they would lose the equity in their homes to staging fights by black youth to feed off the fear that danger was growing in the neighborhood.[3, 8]

In May of 1962, Mayor Daley's Commission on Human Relations recommended that property owners place a signed three-by-five-inch card next to their doorbells, stating clearly that they were not interested in selling their home. Real estate agents were going door to door to generate panic; if they ignored these cards, they gave the owner of the property grounds for a complaint to licensing authorities.[32] One of the more successful neighborhood associations managed to get two South Side real estate salesmen sentenced to prison for "conspiring to cheat and defraud two families in a house deal in a changing neighborhood." They also got a realtor fined for harassing white homeowners.[22] Realtors were apparently not always proud of their actions, sometimes operating under false names or changing their company names often.[8]

In 1971, the posting of "For Sale" signs was banned in the City of Chicago, as an attempt to thwart blockbusting and white flight. After a lengthy legal battle, the Illinois Supreme Court ruled such bans were unconstitutional. On a national level, in 1977, a similar ban, whose goal was to prevent white flight in New Jersey, was ruled unconstitutional by the U.S. Supreme Court. However, the Court later upheld a ban in Los Angeles (1984) that was part of a city beautification plan. Chicago passed another ban in 1985; within six months a federal judge had issued a restraining order to stop its enforcement. Although they have been considered by the courts as a restriction of free speech on multiple occasions, many communities have informally enforced bans on For Sale signs over the years, claiming they detract from the appearance of the neighborhood and lower property values.[33-35]

Neighborhood Associations

One researcher of this era called the actions of whites "collective irrationality"—the individual family's decision to move may have been rational, but the overall impact hurt everyone.[36] The white families in St. Felicitas were mostly second-generation immigrants and their only wealth was in the value of their homes; it would be difficult for them to take the message of the blockbusters lightly. Some of them understandably became involved in neighborhood associations in hope of staying in their homes. Here I've provided summaries of a few of the associations active in Chicago in the 1960s, focusing primarily on neighborhoods close to mine.

Hyde Park

From about the 1930s, Chicago's Black Belt included the neighborhoods of Grand Boulevard and Douglas. The area was dubbed Bronzeville by a black newspaperman who felt it better described the skin tone of its residents.[37] The Black Belt eventually grew to include Oakland and extend into Kenwood. South of Bronzeville was Hyde Park. Hyde Park is touted today as one of the "most racially and economically integrated urban communities in the United States."[38] It has been the home of the University of Chicago since the late 1800s. When the Black Belt started to expand into Hyde Park, the Hyde Park-Kenwood Community Conference set out to "manage" its integration. The University of Chicago also funded a new group, the South East Chicago Commission, which worked to enforce building codes and eventually attracted millions of federal dollars for urban renewal. Urban renewal tore down "substandard" housing in the community, displacing low-income residents, most of whom were black. The university also formed its own police force, and both neighborhood associations worked actively on anticrime programs.[36]

The University attracts students, professors and researchers, who, in the fifties and sixties, would have been predominantly white. The neighborhood is also close to Chicago's downtown, borders the lakefront, and has beautiful, older homes. All of these features worked, in conjunction with urban renewal, to keep Hyde Park predominantly white and definitely middle, if not upper-middle class. Although some credit this to the work of the neighborhood associations, they were certainly aided by the presence of the University. The continual demand for housing by white students and professors protected Hyde Park from the pressures that were felt in other South Side neighborhoods, as the black population continued to grow, along with their need for safe and affordable housing.

Woodlawn

When urban renewal displaced poor blacks in Hyde Park, the most likely next step for them was Woodlawn, on its southern border. The neighborhood was 60% white in the early 1950s; by the early sixties it was 95% black.[39] Then the University announced its plan to expand into Woodlawn, removing more low-income housing. There the University faced a strong adversary – The Woodlawn Organization (TWO). TWO was started by church leaders with the backing of the Archdiocese of Chicago. They recruited Saul Alinsky to run it. Alinsky was a Chicago native who had a national reputation for community organizing. In the 1940s, he had organized residents of the South Side's Back of the Yards neighborhood to advocate for better housing and improved city services. His style was abrasive and his methods confrontational, but, when combined with the support of religious leaders, they were effective in Woodlawn. Eventually, an agreement was reached that kept the University from expanding beyond 61st Street, protecting housing in Woodlawn. TWO went on to other issues facing this now low-income community, like unscrupulous landlords and substandard schools. TWO is very different from the other community groups discussed here. They were not focused on integration; the neighborhood had already re-segregated with a black majority. What they were fighting were the ghetto conditions that other neighborhoods feared would befall them, if their efforts toward "successful" integration failed.[5]

South Shore

Bordering Woodlawn on its southeast corner is South Shore, a neighborhood just over a mile north and east of St. Felicitas School and sharing part of its southern border with our neighborhood, Avalon Park. There, the South Shore Commission would become the largest community organization in the country. It was founded in the fifties when it seemed inevitable that the neighborhood would be in the path of the expansion of the Black Belt.[16]

Sociologist Harvey Molotch studied the South Shore Commission's work between 1965 and 1967, while he was a graduate student at the University of Chicago. Molotch reports that, in its early days, the Commission was a split between what he labeled the exclusionists, who wanted to keep blacks out of South Shore, and the integrationists who believed they should work towards "stable" integration. Until 1963, the power in the Commission had been held by prominent businessmen who were mostly exclusionist. For example, one early strategy was to form a syndicate to buy real estate to prevent it from being sold or rented to blacks. The Commission had the support of local politicians and the press; its leaders were well connected to both.[16]

When keeping the neighborhood all white was no longer possible, their goal became to attract middle-class blacks, not "welfare types." Integration now was viewed as a "necessary strategy" for the preservation of the community. The Commission established a tenant referral service, which for a time was the only practical way to find an apartment in South Shore. Applicants paid a fee for the service, which included the cost of a credit check. A staff member then paid the prospective tenants an unannounced visit – to see if the conditions of their current home were up to its standards. The staff inspected their housekeeping but was mostly looking for "overcrowding and communal living," which were felt to indicate "undesirables."[16] Those were, of course, the conditions in the Black Belt that its residents were trying to escape by moving to South Shore.

The Commission denied that they were discriminating; they were just enforcing a policy of "managed integration" with a goal of 50/50, which required "setting up artificial restraints until such a time as the community can achieve racial stability by normal population turnover." Although they were clearly in violation of the Chicago Fair Housing Ordinance, the referral service had not been the subject of review by any public agencies or tested in court at the time of Molotch's study. Even the Chicago Commission on Human Relations was looking the other way, because the goal of the referral service was integration.[16]

Molotch reports no panic-peddling by realtors, no violence beyond minor gang activity, nor whites fleeing South Shore. When he concluded his study in 1967, his data showed that people were moving in and out of the neighborhood at rates that were comparable to such movement in other places. The reason the neighborhood would eventually become all black, per Molotch, was that whites were more interested in living elsewhere, while there was a high demand in South Shore for housing by blacks. His conclusion about the South Shore Commission and similar efforts was that they "not only [do] not succeed, [they are] dangerous. At a minimum, it appears to be a lot of work for nothing."[16]

A very different perspective of the racial re-segregation in South Shore can be found in Caryn Amster's touching memoir about the murder of her father there is 1970. Her conclusion: "Our beautiful, ethnically diverse neighborhood lay wounded at the hands of greedy realtors. We were gullible and they were relentless. We were cowards and they grew rich." Although here she places the blame squarely on realtors, violence in her neighborhood was a big factor. She names the Blackstone Rangers specifically and says that: "By the end of the 1960s, [they] had South Shore choking on fear of its life." Her father's killer was a member of the Blackstone Rangers who was robbing her family's toy store to raise money for their leader's bail.[24]

Auburn-Gresham, aka St. Sabina Parish

West of my neighborhood, past Chatham, is Auburn-Gresham. In her 1995 dissertation, historian Eileen M. McMahon tells the story of the Irish Catholic parish there during racial transition. Her research centers on St. Sabina, whose pastor played a key role in creating The Organization of Southwest Communities (OSC). The OSC was also endorsed by Cardinal Meyer, then head of the Catholic Church in Chicago. The OSC comprised at least twenty neighborhood associations, which made agreeing on an agenda difficult. Monsignor Egan, who ran the Catholic Church's Office of Urban Affairs, said that some of the individual organizations within OSC included racists as members and "had no other function in life except to keep black people out of the community." When deciding on its boundaries, however, one largely black neighborhood was included, indicating that the OSC would not itself be a protective, segregationist group. One of their strategies, however, was to make loans to help whites who wanted to buy or improve homes there after the area was redlined.[22]

The fight for an open occupancy law in Illinois split the OSC. When it was determined the organization would take a stand in support of the law, many from its more conservative faction left the group. McMahon concludes that the OSC ended up confusing everyone—some thought it was segregationist others thought it was communist. The OSC appears to have at least slowed the rate of change from mostly white to mostly black. Compared to the more typical two years, in St. Sabina it took over ten years, giving residents time to learn from each other and have a more positive experience of the racial change than in those neighborhoods where the change was quick.[22]

The parishioners at St. Sabina were tied to their parish the same way that we were to St. Felicitas, so they did not want to "flee" to the suburbs. McMahon quotes one resident of that era who said: "Then just all of a sudden . . . Everybody was saying they were going to stay and then they all left." After a white teenager was fatally shot by a black teenager near St. Sabina's church, the exodus began in earnest. Like us, St. Sabina's parishioners felt they had "lost" their parish. Some blamed the blacks who moved in, others blamed whites who left. Many blamed their pastor, who they felt had encouraged the change by welcoming black families into the parish. He was hurt deeply by letters they wrote expressing this sentiment and the fact that many moved away without saying goodbye to him.[22]

Avalon Park, aka St. Felicitas Parish (and its neighbor, Chatham)

In the summer of 1962, a half-hour documentary aired on a local television station in Chicago titled "Decision at 83rd Street." The 83rd Street reference in the title is the southern boundary of Marynook, that suburb-like quadrant of Avalon Park introduced in Chapter 2. Marynook, just one block from my house, was the focus of the program, which addressed the issue of whether or not blacks and whites can live together in an integrated community. At the time, only two black families lived in there, but eleven more would be moving in soon.[27]

In the film, a white couple living in Marynook tells about getting numerous phone calls from realtors, encouraging them to sell. A white realtor, also living in Marynook, says he is working with the Marynook Homeowners Association to keep the homes attractive to white buyers and avoid the neighborhood becoming rundown. The realtor felt that whites who were moving out were not prejudiced, just feared the potential for decline, as well as a fear that the neighborhood would become *all* black. One of the two black couples then living in Marynook was interviewed for the show, and said they felt welcomed by their white neighbors.[27]

The documentary contrasts the "decision" facing Marynook with the experience of Chatham, the neighborhood just west of ours, where I took swimming lessons. It was on the other side of the Illinois Central Railroad tracks from Avalon Park. Chatham had already "turned," the slang used at the time for going from predominantly white to predominantly black. Residents in Chatham had formed a neighborhood association to try to encourage whites to stay but had failed. The narrator of the documentary uses the word "panic" and says that the changeover in Chatham happened within two years. Several black residents of Chatham are interviewed at their homes and go out of their way to show how the neighborhood is still attractive and has even improved, with property values going up, since blacks moved there. A black minister explains: "The colored are looking for decent homes, a responsible community and to be unnoticed."[27]

The last person interviewed in the documentary is Monsignor Walsh of St. Felicitas. He appears to be uncomfortable and, in my opinion, does not say anything definitive, using phrases like "working hard," "parish spirit," "have been prepared." Unlike the protestant ministers interviewed for the program, he never uses the words "integration" or "Negro."[27]

In 1963, two articles were published in Catholic newsletters that also discuss Marynook. The articles are titled: "How Marynook Meets the Negro" and "They Chased the Gloom Peddlers out of Marynook." They describe efforts by the Marynook Homeowners Association, whose leaders claim to be open to integration and were clearly trying to discourage white flight. One of their strategies was to overtly recruit white families to move into the neighborhood, a practice that would certainly be illegal today. One of the articles addresses this directly, saying "It required careful phrasing, often achieved through trial and error, to explain both to Marynook and to outsiders that in actively seeking white buyers the community had no intention of discriminating against Negros, but rather wanted to balance the picture." The Association's efforts were considered successful at first, as a few white families bought homes in Marynook after the first black family moved in, which was highly unusual at the time.[25, 26]

Being Catholic publications, it is not surprising that one of the articles discusses involvement of church leaders in the effort to stabilize the neighborhood. It mentions our pastor, Monsignor Walsh, specifically:

> "The Catholic pastor in the community, Monsignor James Walsh, has done much to influence the Catholics in Marynook with sermons and a pastoral letter on interracial justice in housing."[26]

The early success of the Marynook Homeowners Association was picked up as a story of national significance in 1965. That summer an article appeared in newspapers in multiple cities around the country, lauding Marynook as an example of successful integration. One paper used the headline "Fight Ghetto, Not Negro Idea Saves This Suburb."[40]

Despite the publicity, blockbusters continued to move in, using mailings, phone calls and door-to-door visits to scare more white homeowners into selling. One mailing said: "Don't panic – the move is on! Your neighborhood is changing, slowly but surely." Their goal, of course, was to *cause* panic. This mailing was the subject of a grievance to the government agency that regulated real estate sales, and the realtor involved was threatened with loss of his license.[25]

An umbrella group that included Marynook, the rest of our neighborhood, and then some, was the Southeast Community Organization, SECO. Our Monsignor Walsh helped to found it in 1961 and was named their man of the year in 1965. Mayor Daley attended a SECO meeting in 1962 and promised that city services in the area would be continued. (It was common belief that services would be reduced when a neighborhood was integrated.)[41] I have vague memories of SECO being mentioned either by my parents or others in the parish, but I was quite surprised to find this notation about it in a church bulletin from 1963, which is repeated here from Chapter 1:

> The South East Community Organization is determined to keep our Community, Marynook, North Avalon, South Avalon, and East of Stony Island Avenue, stable. Its various Committees on Building Code, Public Information, Law Enforcement, Real Estate are working hard and will produce splendid results. There is no need for panic or hysteria. Many homes in our Community are being sold to new parishioners of Saint Felicitas Parish. The best salesmen of our fine residential area must be its confident residents. St. Felicitas is the Patron of our Parish and we have put her in charge of the Community. St. Felicitas and her seven sons will not let us down. And neither should you. We place everything in the hands of God with St. Felicitas and her Seven Sons "packing a big wallop."

In the same bulletin is a listing about the neighborhood group that would have included the church property itself, The South Avalon Community Organization. The bulletin, which I presume was either written by or at least approved by Monsignor Walsh, congratulated the group on its recruiting effort and said this about their upcoming meeting (also repeated from Chapter 1):

> The people of South Avalon are determined to keep and improve their Community. They fear nothing and will combat block busters, avaricious realtors, false rumors, and violators of the Building Code. Your help is needed. It is your civic duty to attend this meeting.

It is difficult to read these excerpts from our church bulletin all these years later without feeling that our parish was up to something at least unseemly, if not outright racist. In her book, "Black Picket Fences," based on research in our neighborhood, sociologist Mary Patillo-McCoy describes SECO and Monsignor Walsh in a positive light, pointing to realtors as the villains in this story.[11] Part One of this book gives my view of what eventually happened to Avalon Park and St. Felicitas Parish.

The West Side

The phenomenon of the neighborhood association was not unique to the South Side of Chicago. It was happening in other cities and on Chicago's West Side, which had an all-black section close to the Black Belt. The United Property Group (UPG) there grew out of violent reactions to the presence of blacks, such as the fire bombings that were not uncommon on the West Side in the late 1950s. The UPG was unsuccessful, but only after trying various legal means to fight laws that would allow integration. They never explicitly stated this as their goal, using instead the code words of the day – stopping blight, protecting property values, improving the community. They also used tactics similar to those already mentioned, such as posting "not for sale" signs next to doorbells; at one point West Garfield Park was said to have had 4,000 such signs.[8]

Historian Amanda Seligman describes the West Side as politically powerless, feeling Mayor Daley favored the South Side, where he grew up. West Side neighborhood concerns were ignored and the area was allowed to decay. African Americans who moved there found an already declining environment with decreasing employment opportunities.[8] The West Side was also hit much harder by the riots of the 1960s and is home to some of Chicago's toughest neighborhoods today.

Successful Groups – Oak Park & Beverly

Oak Park is a suburb not very far west of Garfield Park on Chicago's West Side. It has been described recently as a "beacon of diversity." Legally separate from Chicago, Oak Park passed its own open housing ordinance in the late 1960s. A community relations committee was formed, both to welcome black newcomers and monitor the practices of realtors.[3] A strategy adopted in 1972 included a ban on For Sale signs. Blockbusters had been putting signs on homes that were not for sale – just to convince people that the neighborhood was "changing." To add to the ruse, the realtors would hire black actors to walk around pushing baby strollers.[42]

Despite their being outlawed by the U.S. Supreme Court in 1977, Oak Park still has a ban on For Sale signs in its municipal code. It is legally unenforceable, but realtors have agreed locally not to use signs. Diversity is viewed as an asset in Oak Park today; the fight there was pro-integration, and it seems to have worked.[42] Like Hyde Park, discussed above, Oak Park has many beautiful features, including a collection of homes designed by famed architect Frank Lloyd Wright.

A little closer to St. Felicitas is a similar story – in the neighborhood of Beverly. Several families seeking to get away from the violence in our neighborhood moved there in the late 1960s. The houses in Beverly were larger and more expensive than those in St. Felicitas. Beverly has been described as a neighborhood that "bucked the trend of white flight." When the panic peddlers arrived, homeowners organized to let them know they were not selling.[3]

The lead organization of Beverly's community and homeowners associations, the Beverly Area Planning Association (BAPA), was formed in the forties but was mobilized and strengthened in the early seventies to fight the blockbusters. BAPA did not allow "For Sale" signs and went a step further by suing realtors for steering only blacks to the neighborhood in the 1980s. They also worked to keep the nearby commercial streets vibrant, something that did not happen along Stony Island near St. Felicitas.[36]

Beverly also benefited from Mayor Daley's 1976 decree that all city employees must live within the city limits. Beverly was still in the early stage of integrating then and in a perfect position to be a desirable choice for white city employees. As a result, white flight was slowed and property values climbed as demand exceeded supply.[36]

In 1970, when white families from St. Felicitas were moving to Beverly, it was 99% white; in 2014 it was 62% white.[43] Blacks moved in as they were able and so did whites. This statistic refutes the "tipping point" theory developed in the 1950s, which held that the majority (in this case white) residents all leave when the minority population (in this case black) climbs to between 15 and 30 percent.[36] Some of my friends whose families moved there in the sixties are still there today and raised their own families there.

Concluding Thoughts

Families might have moved away from St. Felicitas, regardless of the racial changes—eventually. Some might have moved because they could now afford newer homes in more affluent neighborhoods or the newer, and cleaner, suburbs. Some really needed bigger homes to hold their large families. Even those families, like mine and those of my friends, who I absolutely believe would have stayed, at least until we finished high school, might have downsized once the kids were all gone. My dad still had that Oklahoma promise to my mom to make good on. I think it is telling, though, that a study set in our neighborhood showed many of the families who had moved in when the whites left in the 1960s were still living there as of the 1990s.[11] A news article in 2004 told of successful blacks in their thirties moving back to the neighborhood when their parents retired because "we didn't want to see just anybody move in to our house." Many of those young people were St. Felicitas graduates, and they described the neighborhood as "a community of hardworking, neighborly families."[44] Middle-class black families have other choices now; St. Felicitas was a neighborhood worth staying in.

So, what can we make of these "community organizations" that were trying to "manage" and "balance" integration? I've tried to view their actions in the context of the era in which they happened. Like me and my friends, white adults wanted to stay in their homes and were worried that integration would mean that they could not. That may have been based on racist beliefs, or maybe it was just based on what they saw happening in other parts of the city. Some of their efforts seem okay to me—fighting the panic-peddlers, encouraging whites to stay. But it appears that most, if not all, of these community groups got their start trying to keep blacks out of their neighborhoods and later worked actively to keep them from becoming the majority. Chicagoans in the sixties might have considered that reasonable, but there is no way I can view it as legal, let alone ethical, moral or honorable now.

My friends and I knew nothing of Marynook's national press or the looming "Decision at 83rd Street" when we were growing up, nor of the work of SECO or similar organizations in other South-Side neighborhoods. Our parents did not discuss such things with us, and we were busy, well, just being kids. Maybe it is the early "success" of these efforts by grownups that kept our neighborhood relatively calm in the early sixties. The "trouble" didn't start for a few more years. Their work may or may not have been well-intentioned, but it was futile.

CHAPTER 8

THE CATHOLIC CHURCH & VATICAN II

Catholic parishes like St. Felicitas were part of a cultural tradition that followed European immigrants to the United States. Some places in Europe used parishes instead of towns to define populations because all, or at least most, of the people in the area were Catholic. The Catholic Church intentionally duplicated this system in the U.S. to help ease the immigrants into their new country and to create strong ties between them and their parishes. Customs from the old country were continued, also, like the parish events and street parades of my childhood. When the Irish began immigrating en masse to Chicago, the archdiocese requested priests from Ireland. The connection to parish grew even stronger with familiar priests who stayed in the parish for many years.[7] This system had a significant influence on Chicago where, in 1910, 90% of residents were either immigrants or their children—and the majority of them were Catholic.[6]

Every parish in Chicago had a grammar (elementary) school and parishioners were strongly encouraged to send their children there. Although the schools were private (they received no tax dollars), tuition was kept affordable. In the early 1960s, the archdiocese set a maximum rate of $60 per child or $100 per family. At one time, Chicago had the largest parochial school system in the world.[22] Parish members were required to raise money, both to subsidize the low tuition and for building projects. In addition to the church and school, a convent and a rectory were needed for each parish. This significant investment in real estate gave parishioners a strong sense of ownership, and kept Catholic parishes from being as mobile as protestant congregations.[7]

When asked where they were from, Chicagoans of my generation, and a generation or two prior, usually gave the name of their parish, not that of an official Chicago neighborhood. To us, the parish was the neighborhood. This sense of ownership, however, sometimes led to territorialism in the ethnic neighborhoods of Chicago. Eventually, through intermarriage and relocation, it became easier for whites to be accepted in a parish of a different European ancestry, as happened in my neighborhood, where many Germans, Polish and Italians were part of a traditionally Irish parish. Blending in was not as easy for African Americans.

Integration

This strong attachment to the parish often created a resistance to intruders, particularly blacks, who did not fit the image parishioners had of their community. Violence against blacks on Chicago's South and West side in the late 1940s was often led by white Catholics. The leadership of the church was at a loss on how to support integration without losing their parishes, so provided little guidance at first, and some Catholics believed the Church supported segregation.[7] But many Catholics were concerned with interracial justice; in 1945, the first Catholic Interracial Council (CIC) was formed in Chicago. It was not part of the archdiocese but was recognized by the Church. The CIC had a goal of ending all forms of discrimination, following a statement by Pope Pius XII that named racism as "the outstanding heresy of the age."[22]

When a few black families moved into the Trumbull Park Homes in the mid-fifties, white crowds protested violently for months. Trumbull Park was in South Deering, a heavily Catholic neighborhood. At St. Kevin's church, just two blocks away from Trumbull Park Homes, whites were seen physically sliding down the pew to avoid black families in church, and boys from St. Kevin's school were caught vandalizing the cars of the black

156

families attending mass.[7]

In 1958, the American Bishops issued a statement titled "Discrimination and Christian Conscience," which condemned segregation; the bishops felt the thousands of individual parishes in the U.S. needed clear guidance. Bishops in the South opposed the statement but were quieted by Pope Pius XII, who wrote a letter of support and made sure it was issued before his imminent death.[7] Pope Pius's successor, Pope John XXIII, surprised many when, less than three months after his election, he called for an Ecumenical Council of the Vatican (Vatican II) because he felt it was time to "open the windows and let in some fresh air."[45] Chicago's Cardinal Stritch also died that year and was succeeded by Cardinal Meyer, who came to Chicago hoping to find a way to stop white flight and the violence related to racial integration.[7]

By the end of 1961, community organizations like those discussed in Chapter 7 were forming all over the South Side, many with financial support of Catholic churches. Catholic priests often played key roles in these groups, such as that played by Monsignor Walsh in SECO. The Church also held political power. Priests had close ties with local politicians; many were their parishioners. The Archdiocese of Chicago was one of the largest owners of private property in Chicago. Since white Catholics tended to stay in their neighborhoods longer than non-Catholic whites, they became a larger majority of the population within the city limits. In some parts of Chicago, at the end of the 1950s, 70% of the population was Catholic.[7]

Despite those growing percentages, the actual number of Catholics within each parish began dropping. Once integration became inevitable, parishes started to believe that their survival might depend on converting the new residents of their neighborhoods. In 1960, Cardinal Meyer called 1500 priests to a conference on "The Catholic Church and the Negro in the Archdiocese of Chicago." He asked the priests to "remove from the Church on the local scene any possible taint of racial discrimination and racial segregation" and emphasized the need for strong conversion programs. Meyer also supported efforts to integrate the informally segregated Catholic high schools on the South Side.[7]

In his autobiography, Father Tracy O'Sullivan, a Catholic priest who served on the South Side in the 1960s, tells of the development by two priests of "The Chicago Plan." The plan was essentially a strategy to encourage non-Catholic blacks to send their children to Catholic schools, which were known for quality education. In return for their children being accepted into Catholic schools, black parents were required to attend Mass with their families on Sunday and take adult catechism classes. O'Sullivan says that this helped to fill the schools and that many blacks converted to Catholicism.[6]

The Civil Rights Movement

The Civil Rights Movement inspired Catholics in Chicago to take a more active approach to social issues, and some began advocating for the rights of blacks to live anywhere in the city they wished. In 1962, a few Catholic lay people from Chicago traveled to the South to participate in racial protests; before this Catholics had not been a visible part of the Civil Rights Movement. This exposure opened their eyes to discrimination within the church. In 1963 a protest was held at a Catholic women's club in Chicago that did not allow black members. Nuns wearing their religious habits appeared in newspapers holding signs condemning discrimination. Some Catholics criticized the nuns for this, saying it was not a place where they should be involved.[7]

Pope John XXIII's Ecumenical Council (Vatican II) finally got underway in October of 1962. Chicago's Cardinal Meyer was one of the clergy selected to participate. At the same time, the Civil Rights Movement was gaining strength in the United States. In January of 1963, the first National Conference on Religion and Race was held in Chicago, with representation from 67 different religious organizations. The Reverend Dr. Martin Luther King, Jr. appeared and told the gathering that the Catholic Church had not done enough in support of Civil Rights. This appears to have been a turning point, as many priests, as well as Catholic laypeople, joined King's March on Washington later that year. A group of twenty five priests met after the march to discuss the need to increase the Church's involvement with the Movement.[7]

In the midst of this activity in the U.S., Pope John XXIII issued the Pacem in Terris (Peace on Earth) encyclical, which included a condemnation of racial discrimination (April 1963). He died just two months later. Cardinal Meyer was part of the conclave that elected Pope Paul VI to replace him. In the fall of 1964, the new pope met with Reverend King and asked him "to tell the American Negroes that [I am] committed to the cause of Civil Rights in the United States." Catholic leaders at all levels now officially condemned segregation. Priests from 59 different American dioceses participated in King's march in support of voting rights in Selma, Alabama in March 1965. At the same time, a group of nuns in Harlem staged their own march, in sympathy with Selma. The media covered both protests, with priests and nuns clearly visible in their religious attire.[7]

Vatican II

Several months after Selma, Pope Paul VI brought Vatican II to a close, after three years of work by thousands of bishops. Vatican II resulted in a series of changes that would "alter Catholic life more dramatically than any set of events since the Reformation" in the sixteenth century. In addition to those changes visible to me as a child, there was a significant change in church doctrine—"from an institution set apart from the world to one intimately concerned with modern life" and in structure from a hierarchical to a servant church. Catholics were told to reevaluate their role in society—and the racial issues front and center in the U.S. gave them an obvious place to engage this new spirit.[7]

The new spirit was not immediately embraced by everyone within the church. Some of the older clergy remained focused on the sacraments and conversion programs, while younger priests were more interested in social justice issues, volunteering for posts in the inner city. Nuns were also moving into the inner city; by 1966, 800 Chicago nuns were involved in the Urban Apostolate of Sisters, which tutored disadvantaged students. Five nuns and seven priests were arrested protesting de facto school segregation, again with news coverage that included photos of them in religious garb. Letters to Chicago newspapers showed strong reactions—both in support and against them.[7]

The Civil Rights Movement needed Catholics in Chicago because of the power held by the archdiocese, but many old-fashioned Catholics felt the church's involvement was a disgrace. Others began to question how the church could suggest that African Americans convert to Catholicism, while white Catholics were resisting integration. The rate of conversion was also declining, with African Americans questioning the lack of black clergy.[7]

The Chicago Freedom Movement

In January of 1966, during what appears to have been a turbulent time within the archdiocese, Archbishop Cody, who succeeded Meyer in 1965, met with Reverend King, who was looking for a place to stage his first protest in the North. Cody decided to distance himself from King, due to rumors of his communist sympathies, but agreed to support his Chicago Freedom Movement. At a kickoff event at Soldier Field, Cody directly linked Vatican II with Civil Rights, calling both part of a "gigantic social revolution."[7]

Many Catholic priests, nuns and laypeople joined in King's march through heavily Catholic Gage Park, but there were also Catholics among those who reacted violently to the march. This was a neighborhood where many whites had moved to escape the expanding Black Belt; they did not want to move again. Religious marchers were targeted by Catholic protesters, who called out things like "You're not a real priest." The crowd even cheered when a nun was hit by a rock and fell. People carried signs protesting "Archbishop Cody and his Commie Coons." The head of the CIC in Chicago was at a loss, saying: "They consider themselves good

Catholics, yet utterly reject integration. And they are particularly bitter toward priests, bishops . . ." The strong neighborhood identity that had been encouraged by the Catholic Church had proved more resistant to change than some of the laws King was protesting in the South.[7]

The violent reaction to the marches in Chicago had revealed racism within the Catholic Church. In response, Cody called for education programs both for clergy and parishioners. A different response was seen from Father Francis X. Lawlor of St. Rita's parish, who decided to work to "protect" the Southwest Side. He was instrumental in getting 10,000 people to join block clubs dedicated to "holding the line" at Ashland Avenue. Lawlor wrote a letter to Cody that said in part, "Unless we hold the line at Ashland Ave, it would only be a matter of time till every Catholic parish and school, built at great sacrifice by the people of the Southwest Side of Chicago, would be empty." Lawlor was publicly denounced by liberal Catholics and eventually forced to leave the city by Cody's order. He came back later, without a parish or any support from the archdiocese, to continue to work for what he called the rights of white Catholics to stay in their homes. Lawlor was a hero to those who wanted to keep their neighborhoods white. There were other priests who were also known racists. Monsignor Malloy in St. Leo's parish, for example, at one point redefined his parish boundaries to exclude a portion where blacks had moved in.[7, 22]

The Split

The combination of Civil Rights and Vatican II was leading to a split within the church in the North. While some Catholics were becoming activists for the cause of equality, others were fighting integration in the name of what they felt was a just cause – their neighborhoods. Vatican II's command to think more globally caused a questioning of the very idea of the insular ethnic parish as community, but some Catholics were still more concerned with their fear of plummeting property values and loss of their traditions than discussions of social issues. It seemed to them that the same

Church who once sanctified the idea of the strong neighborhood was now ready to abandon those neighborhoods to integration.[7]

Within the religious community there was also dissent. Some nuns became more interested in working with the poor than in teaching middle-class Catholic children in the parochial schools, long a cornerstone of the Catholic experience. Millions of Americans had been raised in the Catholic school system. In 1964, between 20 and 40 percent of all school children in Philadelphia, Cleveland and Chicago attended Catholic school. The nominal tuition of those schools was dependent on nuns, who taught without salaries. After the 1960s, the number of women choosing this life began to decline.[7]

The existence of large Catholic school systems also affected school segregation in cities. The strong emotional ties that kept white Catholics in racially changing neighborhoods longer than non-Catholic whites resulted in public schools becoming largely African American before the surrounding neighborhood did the same. Catholic schools were more integrated than the public schools that had essentially re-segregated ahead of the neighborhoods.[7] The two school systems existed within the same neighborhoods, leading to conflicts between school children, like the ones we experienced in our neighborhood.

Another split began to develop within the church. Catholics in the suburbs tended to support integration, which was not happening in their new neighborhoods. Those Catholics still in the city feared that the blacks moving in would cause a decline in parish membership, since they were less likely to be Catholic. Just as the real estate within the numerous city parishes began to show its age, the number of parishioners began to drop. This eventually led to nearly empty churches, convents, and rectories with high maintenance expense, at the same time that the need for new churches in the suburbs was growing. Eventually, formerly strong parishes and parochial schools in the city began closing.[7]

Concluding Thoughts

The challenge of integration in Chicago occurred during the heyday of strong Catholic parishes like St. Felicitas, and collided head on with the pronouncements of Vatican II.[7] The result seems now both extremely complex and completely predictable. Many Catholics who tried to maintain their parishes did so by trying to keep blacks out, but I truly believe that some, like my family and those of my friends, were open to living in an integrated neighborhood. What we couldn't see, of course, was that the strengths we saw in our parish would not be so attractive to the black families moving in. In fact, our traditions and ethnic identity were designed to encourage territorialism and I can only imagine how unwelcoming that may have felt to our new neighbors.

Despite conversion programs and the slower movement out by white Catholics, the number of parishioners and parochial school children began to drop as blacks moved into a neighborhood. Lower numbers combined with aging real estate created an economic burden that could not be sustained. The fact that St. Felicitas survived for many more years is testament to the dedicated parishioners and clergy that succeeded that of the sixties. Knowing this causes me to be even more sympathetic to their loss of the parish, set to close in 2019, and the school, which closed in 2005.

Understanding all this does not make it easier to accept the outcome. Psychologists who have studied white Catholics leaving their cherished parishes have compared it to the grief experienced after the death of a family member.[7] That is exactly how it felt—and still feels—to me.

CHAPTER 9

VIOLENCE & THE BLACKSTONE RANGERS

As my story reveals, by the late sixties, the violence in our neighborhood had increased. The tactics of the panic-peddlers escalated, and groups of black teens were seen walking through the neighborhood with baseball bats and chains. I don't know how much of the violence we witnessed was contrived by real estate speculators, but there was plenty of real violence nearby. The white children and black children inside our school mostly got along fine. The black children who moved into St. Felicitas parish and attended school with us were from well-educated middle-class families who were, as a group, more prosperous than the predominantly Irish Catholics they supplanted. Ours was a neighborhood whose poverty rate went down after white flight.[11] The violence was coming from someone else, but who? The answer to that question is difficult to determine fifty years later.

One thing that we can easily verify is that there were street gangs in the neighborhoods surrounding us. Because of their proximity to St. Felicitas, I have chosen to focus on the Blackstone Rangers, which is also the only gang I remember from that time. Although it doesn't directly answer my questions about the violence in my neighborhood, I'm including it here as it adds to the historical perspective of what was going on around us, as we were making our way through St. Felicitas School.

The Beginnings

Chicago has had gangs since before the Civil War. Irish

gangs on the South Side date back to the 1880s and were prone to fighting with other ethnic groups. These gangs had the support of local politicians (also mostly Irish) who they, in turn, helped to re-elect. This legitimacy allowed them to be referred to as "athletic clubs" instead of gangs. One of them, Ragen's Colts, was founded by a Democratic Alderman, Frank Ragen. Mayor Richard J. Daley was a member of the Hamburg Athletic Club, another Irish athletic club, while he was growing up on the South Side. When they found it necessary, these Irish gangs joined with their enemies from other white ethnic groups to battle blacks. This violence against blacks is one factor that led African Americans to start forming their own gangs.[5, 46, 47]

1919 Riots

In the summer of 1919, riots broke out on the South Side that reflected the dismal state of race relations in the city, just as the Great Migration was getting underway. In the two years leading up to the rioting, 24 homes of blacks had been firebombed. The Irish "athletic clubs" had taken it upon themselves to keep their neighborhoods white and the police did little to stop them. The 1919 riots were part of a state of unrest nationally, dubbed "Red Summer." When the veterans returned from WWI, they faced shortages for both housing and jobs. Blacks who had served in the war had returned to find that they were still not accepted as full citizens. Most of the violence that year was from whites attacking blacks but, in some places, including Chicago, they fought back.[12]

One day at the end of July, a young black man, Eugene Williams, strayed into a portion of Lake Michigan that was considered part of a "whites-only" beach on the South Side. Chicago did not have official Jim Crow laws, but, in practice, there were places that blacks were not allowed to go, and this was one of them. A white man began throwing rocks at Williams and other blacks in the lake. Williams drowned. Police were called but refused to arrest the rock thrower. The city erupted for nearly a week. In the aftermath, over 500 people were injured (342 black,

195 white), 38 died (23 black, 15 white) and a thousand (mostly black) were left homeless due to fires. The police, who were both understaffed and openly supportive of the white athletic clubs, were deemed ineffective, and the Illinois Militia had to be called in to stop the fighting.[48]

Historians have noted that the 1919 riots were an early sign of burgeoning black militancy; blacks were no longer willing to acquiesce, as they would have been forced to do in the South. The city formed an interracial commission to study the riots, which demonstrated the growing role of blacks in public life. At the same time, the rioting served to strengthen inter-racial tensions and solidify segregation.[48]

Emmett Till

A significant event of racial violence in 1955 was the murder of Emmett Till. The murder didn't happen in Chicago, but it is part of Chicago's racial history, nonetheless. The fourteen-year-old black youth was living in the Woodlawn neighborhood when, in the summer of 1955, he went to Mississippi to visit family. He was accused of "flirting" with a white woman, a violation of the code of conduct under Jim Crow. Emmett Till was abducted and murdered by the woman's husband and brother-in-law. The two men were tried for the crime but found innocent by an all-white jury. Mrs. Till insisted on an open casket at Emmett's funeral in Chicago; she wanted the world to see what those men had done to her child. Tens of thousands attended the funeral. Photos of the event, including of the young man in his casket, were published in black periodicals and have since become part of history. The crime gained renewed interest in 2017 when the white woman Emmett allegedly flirted with admitted that she had lied about the most sensational parts of her testimony and couldn't remember the rest.[49]

The 1960s

The first two summers of the 1960s brought protests against

the continued segregation of Chicago's beaches. The public beaches were open to all races, but some were still segregated in practice. One of those was Rainbow Beach, where my family went when I was a kid, and my friends and I hung out during the summers after eighth and ninth grade. A protest in the summer of 1960 led to violence by a crowd of whites against a group of blacks, whose "protest" consisted of trying to enjoy a day at the beach. The following year, a series of more official "wade-ins" were held to protest the segregation. The first included 100 protesters, protected by 200 policemen. Eventually, over a series of weeks, aided by the presence of law enforcement, the white backlash diminished, and the beach was considered integrated from that point forward. Fifty years later, a plaque was installed at the beach to commemorate these events, which I had never heard about.[50]

On a sunny weekend in 1967, a University of Chicago graduate student did a count of the blacks at Rainbow Beach. There were several thousand people on the beach and only two were black. The two were black children accompanying white families.[16] Recently, one of my African-American classmates shared with me that he had gone to the beach during the summers that my friends and I went (1968 and 1969), but he didn't stay because he felt threatened and unwelcome by white teenagers there (who were not students at our school).

In the mid-sixties, decades of tension and disappointment erupted into violence in cities across the country. In Chicago, a protest took place outside a fire station in a black neighborhood where all the firemen were white. It was the day after the infamous Watts riots started in Los Angeles. A firefighter, rumored to have been drunk, caused an accident that killed a young black woman during the protest. This triggered rioting on the entire West side of Chicago.[8,15]

Two more riots happened on the West Side the following year. One was triggered when police shot a man in a Puerto Rican neighborhood. In mid-July, police turned off fire hydrants that black youth were using to combat Chicago's oppressive heat. Despite the fact that The Reverend Dr. Martin Luther King, Jr., who was in the city at the time, appealed for peace, the National Guard had to be called. The rioting lasted a week and spilled over into several neighborhoods. The results included two deaths and two million dollars in property damage.[8]

There are brief discussions in Chapters 6 and 8 about the violence surrounding the Chicago Freedom Movement marches in 1966. In Chapter 4, I wrote about the rioting that occurred in 1968 after the Reverend Dr. Martin Luther King, Jr. was assassinated. The King assassination is the only one of these events I remember from that time. Although much of the violence was at least a few miles away from St. Felicitas, it was starting to close in on us and must have seemed endless to the adults who were trying to keep us safe.

The Blackstone Rangers[51]

Much of what is written about the movement of African Americans to cities in the North points out class differences between what has been identified as two waves of immigration. Many blacks who had arrived in the first wave (around WW I) had begun to achieve middle-class status when the second wave (after WW II) moved into the city. Given the legacy of segregated housing discussed in Chapter 6, families from the two waves were likely to have lived in close proximity, but that did not mean they were the same social class. The children of the first wave had grown up educated. Children of the second wave were more likely to have come from impoverished situations on farms in the Jim Crow South, attending the segregated schools that were ruled inferior by Brown v Board of Education in 1954, if they attended school at all. The now middle-class blacks of the first wave did not want to be associated with the second wave. The youth of the second wave would be the primary impetus behind the development of black street gangs.[5]

The Blackstone Rangers were founded by a twelve-year-old kid, Jeff Fort, whose parents moved their ten children up from Mississippi in 1956. One can imagine the circumstances that the

Fort family had endured; blacks in the South were terrorized by another notorious "gang," the Klu Klux Klan. Between the Klan and the Chicago "athletic clubs," these kids had plenty of role models for gang behavior. To add to that, older blacks involved in gambling and drugs sometimes recruited the youth to commit crimes for them, because they were too young to be sent to prison.

Fort, like many poor and rural immigrants, did not fit in at school in Chicago, socially or academically, and eventually dropped out and ran away from home. He spent time in juvenile detention, but always returned to his neighborhood, Woodlawn. He and his friends hung out at the Woodlawn Boys Club, where they were in the "Rangers," a group based on their ages. When they got kicked out of the club, sometime in the early 1960s, they kept the Ranger name, adding to it the name of the street where they hung out, Blackstone—the same Blackstone Avenue that ran right by St. Felicitas School, just about twenty blocks south of them. Jeff Fort and his friends were starting their little gang about the time that my friends and I were celebrating our First Holy Communion. Jeff Fort is only seven years older than us. As this book reflects, St. Felicitas gave us a sense of community. Fort realized that the poor kids in Woodlawn also needed something to feel connected to, and he figured out how to provide it.

A rival gang, the Harper Boys, fought the Blackstone Rangers for territory, (Harper is one street east of Blackstone), but eventually agreed to join them. The combined group kept the Blackstone Rangers name but Bull Hairston, the leader of the Harper Boys, became president. Bull was a few years older than Jeff Fort and had older relatives, role models, in other gangs. Fort was still actively involved, serving as vice-president, and as the leader and recruiter for the younger members.[5,52]

Fort was really good at recruitment. He was a charismatic leader, despite being a short and scrawny kid. Eventually, joining the Stones, as they were commonly called, was the dream of the children of Woodlawn, who would chant "Mighty, mighty, Blackstone," while playing games in the streets. They were impressed by how the gang members dressed—at first wearing white tee shirts, khakis and expensive athletic shoes. Later the Stones took to wearing black leather jackets and red tams. That is how I remember them. The gang members also had money, an obvious attraction to younger kids who didn't see much wealth in their neighborhood. At first, the money was coming from activities that sound very much like organized crime—businesses paying for "protection" and pimps and gamblers paying the Stones a "tax" on their revenues in Woodlawn. The Stones said that they had to keep their neighborhood safe, because the police were not doing it. One of their slogans was "Stones Run It," and they pretty much did.

Unfortunately, the combined Blackstone Rangers was still not the only gang in town. The Devil's Disciples, later known just as the Disciples, or just the Ds, were very close by and sometimes ventured into Woodlawn, which usually led to violence. For much of the sixties, and after, the Stones and the Disciples fought over territory.

No longer being welcome at the Boys Club, the gang needed a place to hang out. They found it in the First Presbyterian Church in Woodlawn. There, the Reverend John Fry gave them nearly free rein of the building, which included offices and a gym. Fry was hopeful that he could channel the power that the Stones held into something more productive—and stop the violence that was by then consuming his neighborhood. Over time, this would lead him to be widely criticized.[5]

Growth of the Gang

The Stones continued to join forces with other gangs, eventually combining 21 gangs into the Ranger Nation, later the Black P. Stone Nation. Depending on whom you ask, the "P" stood for power, peace, progress, prosperity, people or prince. (Bull had nicknamed Jeff the "Little Prince.") Each of the 21 gangs operated its own territory and had their own leader, who was part of the leadership of the Black P. Stones, known as the Main 21. There appears to have been lots of structure, along with rules, dress codes, slogans (many spray-painted on buildings) and discipline.

Every time a small gang joined with the Stones, the gang's territory expanded. By the end of the 1960s it included "7th to 111th and State to the Lake," which, for non-Chicagoans, is most of the South Side. I've seen membership estimates anywhere between 3,500 and 8,000. At some point there were more gang members than Chicago policemen.[5] In a 2007 episode of the History Channel's series "Gangland," a former Chicago police officer admitted that the police were outmanned by the gangs in the sixties, and that the Stones were at one time more powerful than the police.[53]

The GIU and The OEO

In addition to the Disciples, the Stones had another archenemy, a special unit within the Chicago police department called the Gang Intelligence Unit or GIU. Formed in March of 1967, the GIU's stated purpose was to "eliminate the antisocial and criminal activities of groups of minors and young adults in various communities within the city." Their primary target appears to have been the Black P. Stone Nation.

Reverend Fry and the Stones continually argued that they were being harassed by the GIU and that gang members were being arrested without cause. Even Abner Mikva, the U.S. Congressman who represented the district where the Stones operated, said that there were not enough gang members to possibly have committed the number of crimes they were arrested for. Regardless of how much was actual crime versus harassment, most adults in Woodlawn were now afraid of the gang, and even the Congressman said they were not the "civic-minded young reformers" they tried to portray themselves as.[54]

In June of 1967, The Woodlawn Organization (TWO) was awarded nearly $1 million from the United State Office of Economic Opportunity (OEO) to open four job training centers – two for the Rangers and two for the Disciples. (The OEO was part of President Johnson's "War on Poverty.") Private money followed, including assistance from The Xerox Corporation and the

Chicago Urban League. One controversial aspect of the grant was the requirement that gang leaders be employed as instructors. This was requested by TWO, because it was felt that the neighborhood youth would not respect the middle-class professionals (black or white) who would typically be hired for such positions. The criticism came because most of the gang leaders hired had dropped out of school early and were apparently not given training for these leadership jobs. Jeff Fort allegedly had never even learned to read or write.[55]

Any criticism, however, was tempered by the fact that inter-gang violence had declined in the year leading up to the award of the grant. Public opinion of the Rangers had also improved, partly due to a musical production created for them by singer/songwriter Oscar Brown, Jr. One of the 21 gangs within the Stones starred in "Opportunity, Please Knock," which not only played in Woodlawn but was taken to some predominantly white suburbs of Chicago. A subset of the performers, known as The Blackstone Singers, traveled to California to perform in Watts. Ebony magazine wrote a story about them while they were there, and they were invited to sing on national television – on The Smothers Brothers Comedy Hour. I remember seeing them on television. It was surreal; we didn't know what to think. Some of the kids chasing us in our neighborhood were claiming to be part of the Blackstone Rangers at the same time that people outside of Chicago were viewing them as an example of a youth group using the arts to improve their lives.

This string of good behavior didn't seem to last long. Jeff Fort was jailed on murder charges in July of 1967. He was released in September, but then both he and Bull Hairston were arrested for soliciting juveniles to commit murder. Bull was held without bail, but Jeff was released, only to be arrested again in October for murdering a member of the Disciples. Then three of the Main 21 were indicted on rape charges.

1968

My class's big eighth-grade-graduation year—1968—did

not begin well for the Stones. Besides having their leaders in and out of jail, one of their own was shot and killed outside a liquor store after a New Years Eve Party—by a member of the Disciples. Now an all-out war with their rivals was underway. There was even talk of shutting down the job training program temporarily to avoid violence within the facilities they were using. The program's leadership, fearing that the OEO would use even a temporary closure against them, decided to stay open. No one wanted to risk the grant money. A few days later, a seventeen-year-old Stone shot an eighteen-year-old Disciple—inside the job training center in Woodlawn. All told, there were forty-seven incidents of shootings involving teens in the two gangs—**during the first two weeks** of 1968.[5]

Bull Hairston was convicted of solicitation to murder in May of 1968. In that case, a thirteen-year-old shot three drug dealers while they were sitting in a car. One of them died. The thirteen-year-old was paid $1 for his efforts—by Bull Hairston, who wanted the drug dealers dead for selling narcotics in Stones territory without the gang's permission.[5]

The Stones are often given credit for "keeping the peace" in the Woodlawn neighborhood after the assassination of The Reverend Dr. Martin Luther King, Jr. I've even seen them credited, by a former cop, for keeping the entire South Side from rioting that weekend.[53] They did declare a temporary truce with the Disciples at that time and staged a joint peaceful demonstration.[5] Another ex-cop, however, said that most of the damage on the South Side that weekend happened in the Stones territory. He editorialized by saying there was not much to damage there, since the Stones had already burned much of it down.[55] Father Tracy O'Sullivan, who was working in the neighborhood at the time, credits the Stones for keeping the violence, fires and looting out of Woodlawn. He says that they were first praised for this, but then there was a backlash. The GIU and the Mayor did not like the "positive image and potential political power" it gave them.[6]

Around this time, Senator John McClennan of Arkansas got wind of the gang involvement in the OEO grant and decided to investigate through the Senate's Permanent Subcommittee on Investigations, which he chaired. The Woodlawn Organization (TWO), officially in charge of the OEO grant, was accused of allowing the Stones to use the church, where the program was based, to store weapons, smoke marijuana and have sex. Fry admitted the church provided no supervision, believing the Stones should patrol their own. It was also found that little actual job training was going on; the only classes were the occasional dance or music lesson. Some of the employment records were also questioned.[55]

During June of 1968, as my classmates and I were celebrating our eighth-grade graduation with a summer of parties, Senator McClellan and his colleagues conducted nationally-televised hearings. The ongoing tension between the Gang Intelligence Unit of the Chicago Police Department and the Stones was now on public display. The director of the program defended his use of gang members as instructors and claimed they were being harassed by the GIU. The GIU listed the crimes that had been committed by gang members and told of empty classrooms, despite instructors, who were gang members, receiving salaries. A former leader of the Stones told the Senate that the gang was never interested in any job training; they just wanted the OEO grant money for themselves. His testimony also revealed that, in order to bring kids into the job training center to count as program participants, gang members were snatching them from bus stops on their way to public school, threatening to hurt them and sometimes actually hurting them. The kids were then forced to drop out of school, because only drop-outs were eligible to participate in the OEO program. Instead of being trained for jobs, they were used to commit murders, because the youth would get lighter sentences than gang members. Later it was rumored that the police had bribed this witness and others. The former gang members who testified were promised immunity; the Stones claimed they were all lying.[5, 53, 55]

Reverend Fry came forward in support of the gang, saying that he understood their "refusal to go along with a racist system."

Jeff Fort was called to testify. He requested that he first be allowed to question his accusers. When he was told that was not part of the process in a Senate hearing, he and his attorney walked out. At the end of July, Congress ordered the OEO to stop funding the TWO program. The following day Fort was arrested for contempt of Congress. He was released on a $1,000 bond.[5] Fort was eventually convicted of fraud and forgery of payroll records. The conviction was only for a small amount, which got him five years in Leavenworth Penitentiary. To put him away for good, there needed to be something more. There eventually was.[53]

Despite their growing power, the Stones never managed to get the Disciples to join forces with them. Parts of the South Side continued to be a war zone for these rival gangs. In July of 1968, Bull held a joint meeting with the Disciples; several hundred members of each gang were present. Both sides pledged to stop the fighting and again marched in unity through Woodlawn. The truce did not last long. Bull's conviction and incarceration were followed quickly by two more killings, which led the rival gangs to intensify their recruiting at area high schools.[5]

In the fall of 1968, as my St. Felicitas classmates and I began our high school years at various Catholic schools on the South Side, our contemporaries in public school were witnessing a dramatic amount of bloodshed. In the first three weeks of school, 12 boys were killed and 42 were wounded in gang shootings. Some of the shootings happened in school hallways.[5] My sister recalls hearing that a black teenager who sometimes helped a neighbor of ours in her garden had been shot and killed for refusing to join a gang.

By the time my family moved away from Chicago—because it wasn't safe for us to walk around in our neighborhood—parents of public-school children were afraid to even send their kids to school. Adults in Woodlawn didn't feel safe but were afraid to complain because the Stones might retaliate. Remarkably, some people were still giving the Stones the benefit of the doubt, saying they were doing some good things, like helping youth through social programs at various organizations within Woodlawn.

Famous people kept trying to help them, too—Jesse Jackson, Sammy Davis, Jr.—but they couldn't seem to get along with anyone. Shootings in the streets eventually resulted in innocent people, including children, being caught in the crossfire. Now the violence was not just affecting the two rival gangs.[5]

The 1970s – and beyond

In February of 1970, Manny Lazar, the owner of the toy store where my parents shopped for our Christmas gifts, was shot and killed by a member of the Blackstone Rangers. The gang members had been ordered to find money for Jeff Fort's bail.[24] The toy store was in South Shore, a little more than a mile down the 79th street business corridor from my father's grocery store. My dad would have been in his own store that day. My sister and brother-in-law still worked there, too. Although the rest of us were already living in Oklahoma, the three of them hadn't moved yet, because my dad hadn't sold the store—or our house.

In the 1970s, the Stones added drug trafficking to their operations—first marijuana, then heroin, eventually cocaine. Once they started selling it, they started using it, leading to the vicious cycle of addiction.[53] By 1973, all of the original Main 21 leaders had either been kicked out of the Stones, were in prison, or were dead. Reverend Fry got a tip that he would be arrested and left town suddenly.[5]

When Fort was released from Leavenworth in 1976, after serving his time for defrauding the federal government, he had joined the Nation of Islam, changed his name to Malik and changed the name of the Black P. Stone Nation to El Rukins. Malik means king in Arabic; El Rukin means cornerstone. Fort said he had an epiphany about the future of the Blackstone organization when he realized that an actual black stone was the cornerstone of a mosque in Mecca. This religious conversion led to Fort's falling out with two of the other top leaders of the Stones, including Bull Hairston.[5]

Fort was arrested and convicted on drug charges in 1983. While in prison, he devised a method of sending coded messages to the gang using the prison's pay phone. In this way he was able to maintain control of the El Rukin's operations. Eventually, the FBI managed to crack his code, with help from an El Rukin leader looking for some leniency. What they found in those messages changed everything.

The Stones were in touch with Libyan dictator Muammar al-Gaddafi. They had accepted a deal that would pay them $2.5 million to commit acts of domestic terrorism on behalf of the Libyan government. In 1987, Jeff Fort was convicted of conspiring to commit an act of terrorism on U.S. soil. He was finally put away for a very long time. He will be eligible for parole in 2038, when he is 91 years old.[5]

That didn't end the story of the Blackstone Rangers, but I'll end my story here. One postscript, though: In 1988, Bull Hairston was gunned down on a South Side street. Rumor was that he had refused an order from the El Rukins—possibly from Jeff Fort himself.

Concluding Thoughts

Although it doesn't take away the fear we Catholic school kids in St. Felicitas felt, this story that was unfolding nearby makes our experiences look pretty tame. I don't recall knowing of any gun violence in our neighborhood before I moved away. The weapons in my stories are bats and chains which, while dangerous, are rarely deadly. It's difficult to determine when actual gang activity started occurring in our neighborhood. Based on the territory that the Stones were claiming in the late sixties, our neighborhood was certainly not exempt. Maybe we were lucky that none of our classmates got caught in any actual crossfire. One of my African-American classmates, who stayed in the neighborhood until he left for college, remembers a day during high school when he was playing basketball at Avalon Park. Jeff Fort somehow got himself into a game, despite his small stature and lack of athletic skills. At one point, Fort pulled a gun on an opponent. Luckily, someone managed to get to a phone and call the police. My classmate just remembers running all the way home as fast as he could, nonstop. As far as he knows, no one got shot that day.

Our parents, of course, would have been aware of what was happening in Woodlawn, so very close to where we lived. Until a few weeks before we moved, my dad drove my friends and I into that neighborhood for Friday night "socials" at Mt. Carmel High School. I knew who the Blackstone Rangers were but had no idea how much violence they were involved in. Probably, like other things that we normalized as children growing up in the sixties, we knew it factually, but weren't able to make the leap to what it could have meant to us personally. Even if those community groups discussed in Chapter 7, despite the need for housing by blacks discussed in Chapter 6, had managed to keep some South Side neighborhoods predominantly, or even partially, white, I doubt it would have had any effect on the progression of the Blackstone Rangers. Which leads me back to my original premise: the reason my parents and those of my friends left St. Felicitas while we were still in high school was to keep us safe.

Conclusion

KEEPING FELICITAS

Considering my childhood now, with a fuller understanding of what was happening around us, I cannot imagine how my parents stayed in the neighborhood as long as they did, allowing me to walk to friends' houses, hang out in front of retail stores and take buses and trains to other parts of the city. The violence started out slowly and was not quite deadly, but there was definitely danger around us, and we were girls in our early teens, not a demographic known for good judgment. Maybe our parents didn't know the whole story. I know I didn't tell mine everything that happened for fear they wouldn't let me out of the house. I can imagine that they were trying to figure out how to deal with this new reality, perhaps hoping the "trouble" would pass, and we could resume our lives, living in a great neighborhood that was only improved through integration. I would have hoped that.

As I discovered doing this research, there were very good reasons for black families to want to move into our neighborhood in the 1960s. My family, and those of most of my friends, moved into St. Felicitas parish in the 1950s; the houses there were built in the 1920s. Why did we consider it "our" neighborhood? I understand now that the ethnic parishes created by European immigrants two generations before us had intentionally created this feeling, and the Catholic Church encouraged parishioners to take ownership of its small, internally focused parishes. It worked.

Much of what I have read and learned since that time has caused me to accept that our parents and teachers were a product of their own era—struggling to understand what was happening and to assimilate it with their values and beliefs, which had undoubtedly been influenced by the legacy of racism prevalent in America during their lives. Their thoughts and actions during the challenging time discussed in this book were surely not always benevolent, but in the memories of their children, they are still the "good guys" in this story. They didn't run away when blacks moved in and were not out throwing rocks or yelling epithets at the newcomers. More importantly, they never said or did anything to try to influence their children to judge people based on their race. My parents and those of the women who shared their stories for this book didn't, anyway.

You might think that our experience of violence, together with the sense of loss and even resentment at having to move away when we did, would have encouraged tendencies toward prejudice in me and my white grammar school friends. Although I believe everyone harbors some prejudices, it would be almost impossible not to in our society, my group of St. Felicitas friends are actually the least biased people I have ever known. I have met people in my generation who grew up without having met a black person, much less gone to an integrated school, yet they have beliefs about what "they" are like. Getting to know our African-American classmates in St. Felicitas during our grammar school years helped us to accept others as individuals without ascribing them any preconceived notions based on their race.

In 2018, my St. Felicitas classmates held a reunion in honor of the 50th anniversary of our graduation. We have had a spattering of reunions over the years, but not since 1978 have we tried so hard to find everyone in our class and invite them to join us in this celebration. Of the 76 students in our graduation photo, we discovered that 13 have died. Of the remaining 63, we found 50 and 33 attended the reunion, along with eight classmates who had moved away before graduation and several St. Felicitas grads from other classes. It was an amazing experience. We had fun, laughed, cried, and honored the classmates we have lost. I talked to people I hadn't even thought about in fifty years. Boys even. I don't think I ever spoke to the boys in eighth grade. Although I had driven to Chicago from Florida, some 1100 miles, I was not the graduate who traveled the farthest; two flew in from California. Others came from

Georgia, Arkansas, Maryland—and many from Beverly and the south suburbs of Chicago. Fifty years is a long time. Our parents have all passed away and we have had our careers and raised our own families, but we have not forgotten our time at St. Felicitas. Something about it bound us together. Maybe it was the closeness of the community, or maybe it was some sort of post-traumatic stress for having lived through such a fearful time together.

Of the 22 black students who graduated with us, we know that three have died. We were able to locate 11 of the remaining 19, and four of them attended the event. Although I have not kept in touch with my black classmates over the years, I was disappointed not to see more of them at what will most likely be our last reunion. St. Felicitas School closed in 2005. In the years after my family moved away, it saw many classes of predominantly African-American children pass through its halls. Based on their childhood memories (as shared on Facebook!) the school meant just as much to them as it did to the European-American children before them.

The day after our reunion, many of us attended mass at St. Felicitas Church, one of the last to be celebrated there. Sitting in the church again, I had the opportunity to contemplate its beauty one last time. I spent most of the mass feeling nostalgic—thinking of my dad as an usher, my sister as a bride, my friends and I during all those early morning masses before school. Then I came to a realization: Our beautiful old church, like our old school, has had its day. They have done their job and done it well. It is time to let them go.

Our Felicitas now is truly lost, but it will never be forgotten. I know for sure that the class of 1968 has not forgotten Felicitas. We kept her close in our memories and will continue to for as long as we live.

ENDNOTES

1.   Hansberry, L., *A Raisin in the Sun*. 1959.
2.   Bernstein, D., *Martin Luther King Jr.'s 1966 Chicago Campaign*, in *Chicago Magazine*. 2016.
3.   Moore, N.Y., *The South Side: A Portrait of Chicago and American Segregation*. 2016.
4.   *www.upwithpeople.org*
5.   Moore, N.Y.and L.Williams., *The Almighty Black P. Stone Nation - The Rise, Fall, and Resurgence of an American Gang*. 2011.
6.   O'Sullivan, T., O. Carm, *Been There All Along*. 2013.
7.   McGreevy, J.T., *Parish Boundaries: The Catholic Encounter with Race in the Twentieth-Century Urban North*. 1996.
8.   Seligman, A.I., *Block by Block: Neighborhoods and Public Policy on Chicago's West Side*. 2005.
9.   Coates, J., *Riots Follow Killing of Martin Luther King, Jr.*, in *Chicago Tribune*. December 19, 2007.
10. *Screams Repel Assailant*, in *Chicago Tribune*. November 16, 1968.
11. Patillo-McCoy, M., *Black Picket Fences - Privilege and Peril Among the Black Middle Class*. 1999.
12. Grossman, J.R., *Land of Hope - Chicago, Black Southerners, and the Great Migration*. 1989.
13. Wilkerson, I., *The Warmth of Other Suns - The Epic Story of America's Great Migration*. 2010.
14. Manning, C. (2005) *African Americans*. The Electronic Encyclopedia of Chicago.
15. Gartz, L., *Redlined: A Memoir of Race, Change and Fractured Community in 1960s Chicago*. 2018.
16. Molotch, H.L., *Managed Integration - Dilemmas of Doing Good in the City*. 1972.

17.   *Avalon Park.* www.chicagoparkdistrict.com/parks-facilities/avalon-park. Accessed March 13, 2019.

18.   Coates, T.-N., *The Case for Reparations*, in *The Atlantic.* June 2014.

19.   Seligman, A.I. (2005) *Woodlawn.* The Electronic Encylopedia of Chicago.

20.   Nelson, R.K., LaDale Winling, Richard Marciano, Nathan Connolly, et. al. *Mapping Inequality.* American Panorama. https:/dsl.richmond.edu/panorama/redlining. Accessed March 6, 2019.

21.   Satter, B., *Family Properties - How the Struggle Over Race and Real Estate Transformed Chicago and Urban America.* 2009.

22.   McMahon, E.M., *What Parish Are You From?: A Chicago Irish Community and Race Relations.* 1995.

23.   Ralph Jr., J.R., *Northern Protest: Martin Luther King, Jr., Chicago and the Civil Rights Movement.* 1993.

24.   Amster, C., *The Pied Piper of South Shore.* 2004.

25.   Brodkey, N. (1963) *They Chased the Gloom Peddlers Out of Marynook.* New City: Man in Metropolis a Christian Response. www.issuu.com. Accessed January 30, 2018.

26.   Sullivan, T. (1963) *How Marynook Meets the Negro.* www.issuu.com. Accessed January 30, 2018.

27.   WBBM, *Decision at 83rd Street.* 1962, Museum of Classic Chicago Television. www.fuzzymemories.tv. Accessed May 16, 2018.

28.   Brown, F.L., *Trumbull Park.* 1959.

29.   Choldin, H.M. (2005) *Chicago Housing Authority.* The Electronic Encyclopedia of Chicago.

30.   BPI, *Court Approves Settlement In Landmark 'Gautreaux' Desegregation Lawsuit Blocking Racial Discrimination In Public Housing.* www.bpichicago.org/blog. Accessed March 6, 2019.

31. Best, W. (2005) *Avalon Park*. The Electronic Encyclopedia of Chicago.
32. Grimm, R., *Civic Machinery Turns Against 'Panic Peddlers'*, in *Chicago Tribune*. May 6, 1962.
33. Hirsch, A. (2005) *Blockbusting*. The Electronic Encyclopedia of Chicago.
34. Crawford Jr., W.B., *'For Sale' Sign Ban Stopped by Judge*, in *Chicago Tribune*. September 24, 1985.
35. Shaman, D., *Does the First Amendment Protect For-Sale Signs?*, in *New York Times*. November 17, 1996.
36. Taub, R.P., et. al., *Paths of Neighborhood Change - Race and Crime in Urban America*. 1984.
37. Travis, D.J. (2005) *Bronzeville*. The Electronic Encyclopedia of Chicago.
38. University of Chicago. *Pritzker School of Medicine: About Chicago and Hyde Park*. http://pritzker.uchicago.edu/page/about-chicago-and-hyde-park. Accessed March 7, 2019.
39. Breitbach, C. *The Woodlawn Organization*. AREA Chicago. www.areachicago.org. Accessed September 19, 2018.
40. Scherf, M., *'Fight Ghetto, Not Negro' Idea Saves This Suburb*, in *Fort Lauderdale News*. May 14, 1965.
41. *Tell S.E. Side Don't Panic on Racial Issue!*, in *Chicago Tribune*. March 26, 1962.
42. Jackson, S., *Not in Your Front Yard: For Sale Signs are Banned in Oak Park*, on *Curious City*, WBEZ. March 21, 2016.
43. Moore, N., *In Chicago's Beverly Neighborhood, Integration Is No Accident*, on *Curious City*, WBEZ. March 26, 2014.
44. Turner Trice, D., *Pull of home is being felt in Avalon Park*, in *Chicago Tribune*. October 25, 2004.
45. Wikipedia. *Second Vatican Council*.
46. Kass, J., *Gangs that came to rule in seats of power*, in *Chicago Tribune*. June 22, 2012.

47. Diamond, A.J. (2005) *Gangs*. The Electronic Encyclopedia of Chicago.

48. Pacyga, D.A., *Polish Immigrants and Industrial Chicago - Workers on the South Side, 1880-1992*. 1991.

49. McLaughlin, E. and E. Grinberg., *Justice Department Reopens Investigation into 63-year-old Murder of Emmett Till*, CNN, July 12, 2018.

50. Keilman, J., *Rainbow Beach 'wade-ins' broke down racial barrier*, in *Chicago Tribune*. July 10, 2011.

51. Where not otherwise noted, this history is my interpretation of various sources, primarily Moore & Williams, *The Almighty Black P. Stone Nation* (see Endnote 5). Any opinions expressed, however, are my own.

52. Fry, J.R., *Fire and Blackstone, Non-sermons by Chicago's white activist minister*. 1969.

53. Gangland, *Stone to the Bone*, on The History Channel, Season 1, Episode 7. 2007.

54. McPherson, J.A., *Chicago's Blackstone Rangers (Part II)*, in *The Atlantic*. June 1969.

55. McPherson, J.A., *Chicago's Blackstone Rangers (Part I)*, in *The Atlantic*. May 1969.

BIBLIOGRAPHY

Nonfiction – Most Relevant to Losing Felicitas

- The South Side: A Portrait of Chicago and American Segregation – Natalie Y. Moore (2016)
- Black Picket Fences: Privilege and Peril Among the Black Middle Class – Mary Patillo-McCoy (1999)
- Parish Boundaries: The Catholic Encounter with Race in the Twentieth-Century Urban North – John T. McGreevy (1996)
- What Parish Are You From?: A Chicago Irish Community and Race Relations – Eileen M. McMahon (1995)
- The Warmth of Other Suns: The Epic Story of America's Great Migration – Isabel Wilkerson (2010)
- The Almighty Black P. Stone Nation: The Rise, Fall, and Resurgence of an American Gang – Natalie Y. Moore and Lance Williams (2011)
- Block by Block: Neighborhoods and Public Policy on Chicago's West Side – Amanda I. Seligman (2005)

Nonfiction – Less Relevant to Losing Felicitas

- Family Properties: How the Struggle Over Race and Real Estate Transformed Chicago and Urban America – Beryl Satter (2009)
- Land of Hope: Chicago, Black Southerners, and the Great Migration – James R. Grossman (1989)
- Managed Integration: Dilemmas of Doing Good in the City – Harvey Luskin Molotch (1972)
- Northern Protest: Martin Luther King, Jr., Chicago, and the Civil Rights Movement – James R. Ralph, Jr. (1993)

- Paths of Neighborhood Change: Race and Crime in Urban America – Richard P. Taub, et al (1984)
- Polish Immigrants and Industrial Chicago: Workers on the South Side, 1880-1992 – Dominic A. Pacyga (1991)

Fiction

- A Raisin in the Sun – Lorraine Hansberry (1959)
- Trumbull Park – Frank London Brown (1959)

Memoir

- Been There All Along – Tracy O'Sullivan, O. Carm. (2013)
- The Pied Piper of South Shore: Toys and Tragedy in Chicago – Caryn Amster (2004)
- Redlined: A Memoir of Race, Change and Fractured Community in 1960s Chicago – Linda Gartz (2018)

Made in the USA
San Bernardino, CA
02 July 2019